From Soviet Union to USA:

Our Story

By

Alex Nason

From Soviet Union to USA: Our Story

Copyright @ 2019 by Alex Nason

Published in the United States by BCG Publishing, 2019.

"The Soviet Union was in the middle of a tremendous wheat shortage, plus a grain embargo led by the US, and was struggling to find ways to keep its citizens fed.

American politicians seized this opportunity to help Russian Jews escape from the Iron Curtain.

They negotiated a trade with the Soviet government: wheat for exit visas.

Thousands of lives suddenly and unexpectedly changed, including mine.

I still wonder how much wheat my young family's freedom was worth."

Realizing that family history stories our parents and grandparents are telling us don't necessary register and are kept in our brains, is the reason for my memoirs

Table of Contents

About the Author

Alex Nason has retired in 2018, after a successful career as an engineer and a business owner.

Alex Nason was born in Moldova, one of the former Soviet Union states, where he grew up persecuted for being Jewish. At the age of 26, he, his wife and three-year-old son left the Soviet Union seeking a better life.

On January 21, 1981 they arrived to the United States. With major challenges ahead, his journey towards the American dream started on that date. There were no relatives, no friends he could rely on. His English knowledge was limited to less than a few hundred words, and so was the amount of his money.

Life behind the iron curtain left him unprepared for the United States. It was literally back to the drawing board, starting from scratch, including the culture shock he faced in Houston, Texas.

Chapter 1

I was born in the small Moldavian village of Sholdaneshti, about 80 km from Beltsy. We lived in a house together with my mother's parents, who built the house before World War II.

In 1941, as the Germans approached Sholdaneshti, my grandparents and my teenage mom were evacuated from the village and moved to the city of Saratov, about 500 km east of Moscow. After the war, they came back and found the house in good condition. They were among the very few lucky people to have a roof over their heads after returning from the evacuation. My grandfather always told us that the only reason the house hadn't been destroyed was because he buried a Torah under it before they were forced to leave. When they returned almost four years later, the house and the Torah were untouched.

Right after their wedding in 1949, my parents moved in with my grandparents and got two rooms to themselves, leaving two more rooms and the kitchen for my grandparents. There were no bathrooms in the house—we had to use an outhouse in the backyard. The big oven in the kitchen was used to keep the house warm, and it was my preferred sleeping spot during the winter. Every few days, my grandparents baked fresh bread in the oven, and one of the best memories I have about my childhood is that smell of fresh-baked bread.

Our backyard was very big, and all kinds of fruits and vegetables grew there. We also had a cow, a few pigs, and a lot of birds. In the early 1950s, my father used part of our backyard to build a house for his sister.

I was the second child born to my parents; their first child was two years old when he died from meningitis.

My mom was the most educated person in our family. She had eight years of Russian school and worked as a bookkeeper for a state company, Zagodzerno. My dad had only four years of school. At the age of nineteen he was drafted into the army and ended up in World War II fighting for the Russians.

During the war he was wounded eighteen times and was captured by Germans once. Together with another soldier, they escaped by pretending to be dead and lying still under the dead bodies of their friends. My dad received a lot of medals but didn't talk much about the war. He opened up only to Robby, his grandson, telling him the history behind each of the medals. Robby loved it, and that's when I learned a lot about my dad's services during WWII.

The main language spoken in our house was Yiddish, the second was Romanian, and there was almost no Russian spoken. I only started to speak Russian when I was five years old and had to go to kindergarten.

My grandparents were the ones who spent the most time raising me. I was a spoiled child and was also sick very often. I had every possible illness a child can have. I was not a good eater, and everyone in my family, especially my grandmother, tried different techniques to feed me. One of the most memorable was feeding me while I sat on a turntable, and I got a teaspoon of food every time my face was in front of her. The turntables were mechanical, and at the end of each feeding one would break, so they kept at least five new ones in our house at any given time. At that time, my dad was the manager of a large state supply company, and turntables were among the items he stocked.

Every year my grandfather made his own wine. We had two one-ton barrels in the cellar, and I was the one who brought wine to dinner. At the age of seven, I was allowed to have some wine, which didn't have any sugar. It was the fully fermented wine with no residual sugar and no additives added to sweeten in. It tasted like very good grape juice.

When I was almost five years old my parents decided to enroll me in kindergarten, which was only five houses away from our house. On the second day I decided it wasn't for me and tried to escape. It didn't work. On the third day I stood next to the fence and asked adults passing by to take me home, or tell my grandmother to come and pick me up. That also didn't work. On the fourth day, I cried nonstop for the whole day. By the end of the day when my mom picked me up, it marked the end of my kindergarten era.

I tried the same crying technique on September 1, 1960, on my first day of school. I was left with thirty strangers and had to sit for forty-five minutes without moving around, just listening to the teacher. I began crying and stopped only after my dad showed up. I told him that as long as he was with me I would be okay. He stayed in the classroom for the whole day.

The next day we had to repeat the same thing. In the evening my dad told me that was the last time he would attend the school with me. After arguing for a few minutes, for the first and last time in my life, my dad took out his military belt and used it. My behind was sore for a few days, but I got the message and attended school after that without any problems.

Sholdaneshti had a population of approximately 2,000, and there were about fifty Jewish families. Most of non-Jews liked Jewish people; however, there were quite a few who didn't. My grandparents were very religious. Every morning at least ten adult Jews were coming to our house. According to the Jewish law, at least ten Jewish people are required to be present to conduct a communal service, called minyan. I was prohibited from discussing this with anybody outside the house. When I turned thirteen, my grandfather and father helped me put on the tefillin and made me repeat the blessings after them. My mom and grandma cooked food, and everyone who was at our house for the minyan had drinks and food that morning. Again, I was told not to discuss this with any of my friends. Only later in my life did I understand that this was my Bar Mitzvah.

I was fourteen when my family decided to move to a larger city. My dad found a job and bought a three-room condominium on the third floor of a five-story building. As soon as I finished seventh grade, my grandparents and I moved to Beltsy, about 80 km away from Sholdaneshti. Shortly thereafter, my parents sold our house in Sholdaneshti and joined us. The year was 1967, the population of Beltsy was around 100,000, and there were about 3,000 Jewish families there. For me this was a very big change—I didn't know anybody, the few friends I made during my first month there were non-Jews, and most of them didn't like Jews.

The school I was assigned to attend had more Moldavian kids than Russians and Jews combined. I was okay with that because I was fluent in Moldavian and blended in well with the rest of my classmates. However, the day they found that I was Jewish, our relationship drastically changed. At school, and especially on the way home, a group of five or six kids always teased me about being a Jew. Soon it became physical—they pushed me around, and a few times punches were thrown. I was scared, but I knew that if my grandparents found out about this, they would escort me to and from school, trying to protect me. At that time, I didn't have many Jewish friends I could ask for help, so my only solution was to quickly learn how to defend myself.

To my parents' surprise, I told them that I wanted to take freestyle wrestling lessons. Within a week I signed up with the wrestling club and began my training. Many of the students showed up for training two to three times a week; I was there every day. The trainer was very pleased with my attitude and spent a lot of time personally teaching me. I was a quick learner, and at the end of my second month he told me that I'd be competing with the other wrestling club in the city. After that, I still let my classmates push me around, but I felt that I could defend myself much better than I had been able to a few months prior.

Finally, I decided not to take it anymore. When one of my classmates accused me of having stolen his book, he told me that because I was Jewish, I should leave that city and go to Israel. The rest of the group started to scream at me "Jihd," a dirty slang word for Jewish people in Russia. I made a quick decision. I was alone against six kids, and I knew I had to act quickly. As I dropped my backpack, all of them started to laugh, and as one of them tried to punch me, I grabbed his arm, dropped under him and did what I had been practicing every day for the last few months: I picked him up and threw him over. At practice, we would ease the partner's fall to the soft mat; here, I let him fall to the concrete without any protection. As he lay on the ground really hurting, no one moved to help him. While holding him down, I asked if someone else wanted to try to hurt me. I stood up only after all of them moved back, and then I picked up my backpack and walked away. It was the best experience I had ever had in my fourteen years. It felt great to be the winner and to see the fear in my attackers' faces. I was walking away without knowing what to expect next; they could have run after me and easily overpowered and beaten me up in retaliation.

At dinner I told my parents about this incident. My dad and grandfather were very proud and happy about what I had done, but my mom and grandmother were afraid of retaliation.

To my surprise, the next day the guy I beat up came over and told me that he was sorry for his behavior during the last few months. He asked if we could be friends. I didn't expect to hear this from someone who really didn't like Jews, but I learned a very important lesson: bad people respect power. We didn't become friends, but I never again heard the word "Jihd" from him.

I continued to train for another four years, twice winning the junior state championship. Taking wrestling lessons was one of the most important steps I ever took. It gave me confidence for the rest of my life.

Chapter 2

Our Wedding
Dad, Mom, Sophia's Mom, Sophia's Dad
Sophia, me

I was a good student in high school and graduated with A and B grades (5 and 4 in the Russian system). My dad really pushed me to become a medical doctor, but I decided to become an engineer. The nearest college was the polytechnic institute in the capital of our state, Kishinev. It was about 130 km away from home, and that's where I applied upon graduation from high school.

Not going to college was never an option for me because it was my parents' decision long before I graduated from high school. There were two major reasons for this: first, they strongly believed in having a profession backed by a college education; second, they wanted me to avoid the Russian army. The army was mandatory for all men at age eighteen, and the only option to avoid it was by attending a university. Military was taught at the university, and after graduation from college, we were given the rank of lieutenant in the Soviet army. All of us were placed in the army reserve, and only a very few had to go into the regular army.

It was no secret that the Russians had different rules for Jews to be accepted to a college. Regardless of their knowledge, colleges had quotas to accept only a certain number of Jews. The Soviet system of acceptance to a college included passing four different exams—in my case it was math, physics, Russian language, and an essay. Each exam was graded between 3 and 5. A grade under 3 eliminated an applicant. The average exam grade, the background of the applicant, and the applicant's political views were the criteria for the acceptance committee.

After answering all written questions on the math test paper, I sat down with the professor for him to grade my answers. To my surprise, without even looking at my written answers, he started to ask me questions not taught in high school. I didn't know the answers to most of his questions. With a smile of satisfaction, he told me that I didn't pass the math exam and would have to apply for college the following year.

When I tried to appeal his decision I was told that, based on the professor's report, I didn't know the answers to his questions that I should have known. They even had a fabricated list with the questions I supposedly failed to answer correctly. When the appealing committee informed me that they had no reason to believe my story, and my case was dismissed. It was very upsetting, but I was ready to try again the next year. Because I started school when I was six years old, I had one more year to try to get into college before I turned eighteen, the draft age for the Soviet army.

Shortly thereafter, I found a job and started working for a state company doing surveys in small towns. My job required a lot of traveling with overnight stays at those locations. Most of the officials in small towns felt that they had to wine and dine me in order to get favorable surveys. It didn't take long for my parents to realize that this job was not for me, and by the end of the first month they made me quit, simply because I was coming home drunk after the trips.

I was studying most of the time, getting ready for the next year's entrance exams. My parents hired tutors who were teaching me much more than the regular high school required. My dad decided not to take any chances with my second attempt. He found some key people at the university, and in exchange for a large sum of money, got their assurance that I wouldn't be on the list of people who were prevented from entering college. All it meant was that I had to pass the tests and fairly compete with the rest of the people trying to get into college. I think there were about nine or ten kids competing for each available space. This time I passed all four exams and made it into college, majoring in cooling and refrigerating systems.

It was also the time when I fell in love with Sophia. Because she was two-and-a-half years younger than I, she was always just a little girl who was my sister's friend and whose parents were friends with my parents. She was a beautiful girl, and during the year I spent home before attending college, I began to notice her more and more but never asked her out. Only after leaving for college, then returning for my first visit home did I ask Sophia to join me at a party. We had a good time, and shortly thereafter, we began dating.

Our parents were very close friends, but when both of our mothers found out that we were dating, they weren't very happy. My mom was worried that I wouldn't make Sophia happy because she was a spoiled child whose parents had a lot of money and would do whatever she asked them to do. Sophia's mom had similar thoughts about me. On the other hand, our dads had a different opinion, and both were very happy about us dating. As soon as Sophia graduated from high school, she moved to Kishinev, where I found her a place to live; it was in the house sharing the yard with the house I was renting.

When Sophia moved to Kishinev both of us lost interest in studying. We very much enjoyed being together, but that didn't go well with my education; I was skipping classes, couldn't pass the tests, and had no choice but to take a year off. It was almost an impossible task to take a year off at a university, but with my dad's help it was approved, and we moved back to Beltsy. After we moved back, we began discussing marriage, and it didn't take long for our wedding to happen. We were married July 13, 1974, with over 300 guests attending the wedding.

In September we were back in Kishinev as a married couple. Sophia's parents bought a house in Kishinev, and while they were still in Beltsy, Sophia and I moved in. In February of 1977 Robby was born, and in May I graduated from the university with a master's degree in mechanical engineering.

At the same time Sophia also graduated from the Kotovsk College of Civil Engineering, which was a very hard task because Kotovsk was about 20 miles south of Kishinev, Sophia was pregnant, and she had to travel to school at least three to four times a week.

Finding a job after graduating college in the Soviet Union was a simple process. Each college received requests from companies in need of new engineers, and the graduates chose the one they wanted to work for. As a rule, the number of requests was higher than the number of graduates, and the list with the openings was available for the graduates' review a few months prior to graduation. Colleges ranked graduates based on average grades. The highest ranked could choose from the entire list of available jobs, and the last one on the list would have to choose from whatever was left. Our class graduated about seventy people, and based on my grade average I was among the first fifteen people to choose a company. Because all of us knew our rankings it was pretty easy to choose, and we told each other what our choices were. After the people ahead of me made their choices, I chose a company I wanted to work for. My first choice was a company related to the military industry. It had everything I wanted: good pay, interesting research, and, very importantly, the ability to shop at a special grocery store that was closed to the general public. That may sound funny, but the grocery store was an important element in my decision-making because I would then be able to buy necessary food for my family without asking my dad to get it for me.

We were asked to come one by one to the room where the president of the university, the dean of the mechanical department, and the communist and Komsomol chiefs would hand us our diplomas. The job selections were also made there, so by the time we left that room, we had our diplomas as well as a job for the next three years. After receiving my diploma, I let them know which company I chose to work for. To my great surprise, the communist chief immediately told me that the company I had chosen had canceled their request, and the job was unavailable.

There was a very similar position available with another company, and I requested it. This time the university president told me that someone else had already taken that position. I knew that it couldn't be true; none of the people who were ahead of me had chosen this company. When I asked for the name of the person who took this position, he didn't answer. As I looked at their smiling faces, it became very clear to me that the only reason I didn't get the jobs I wanted was because I was Jewish. Even though it was nothing new, it was very hard to accept. Looking directly at the university president, I asked if that was indeed the reason. Was I being punished for being Jewish? He became visibly angry and tried to ignore my question. He advised me not to waste time and to pick another place.

I couldn't be quiet anymore. For the first time, I loudly expressed myself about their policies against Jews and how wrong they were. The communist chief shouted back at me, asking if I was a communist and if my father or grandfather were in the communist party. When I answered "no" to his questions, he told me that I shouldn't expect to work at military-related jobs because it would put me in a better position than graduates whose families were communists. Knowing that our argument was going nowhere, I told them it would be best if they made my job selection with the requirement that the job would be in Kishinev. With smiles on their faces, they told me that the state design company would be a perfect match. This place was almost at the bottom of my list—the projects they were involved in were boring and the pay was not good. Upon receiving my diploma, I immediately left because I was very upset and afraid of getting in trouble by further vocalizing my opinions.

Only a few days later, I found out who got the jobs I had chosen. My first choice job was given to someone who was almost on the bottom of the list but whose father was the Interior Minister of our state. My second choice was given to the son of another state official who didn't study well and was also at the bottom of the list. I was a friend of both of them, had often helped them with their homework, and enjoyed partying with them during our college years. I know they felt bad about all this but were afraid to speak out.

Walking home after receiving my diploma, I began making plans for my family's departure from Russia. I knew that experience was a perfect example of how my family and I would live our lives there. It was scary to think that our newborn son would have to grow up and live in a society that would hate him simply because he was born Jewish.

I was also thinking about my dad. He never joined the communist party but almost lost his life fighting in World War II. That day, all they asked about him was whether he was a communist, even though they had the paperwork for my entire family and knew that he was wounded eighteen times during the war and received numerous medals. As for me, I knew that joining the communist party would never be an option; no matter how hard I worked, my family would never have a good future in the Soviet Union.

I was sure that Sophia would be extremely happy with my decision. She had been thinking and talking about us leaving the Soviet Union for a long time. I was the one who was holding her back, and the biggest reason was my refusal to leave without my parents and my sister. None of them would have minded leaving Russia, but my parents had made it very clear that they would go only if my sister was married first. I also knew that the possibility of seeing

13

my parents again was very low. It was a very tough situation, and I had to make a very hard decision.

Chapter 3

On my way home from the university, I decided for certain to leave Russia for the sake of my own family. When I told Sophia, she was very happy. The next day we went to Beltsy to let my parents know. It was very hard for me to break the news. I remember the expressions on my parents' faces. They were surprised and sad. I can only imagine how hard it was for them to accept and to agree to let us go. What made it a little easier on all of us was that my sister, Polina, had been dating a guy whose brother was already in Israel. It was in line with our plans that if they got married, there wouldn't be any problem for all of them, including my parents, to leave Russia. Polina's boyfriend assured me that he would have no problems applying for visas as soon as the clearance he had obtained in the Russian army expired. He was out of the army for over a year already, so the maximum wait would be another two years.

The biggest challenge, however, was in front of us. We had to have an invitation from a close relative (parents or siblings) who were residing in Israel. In our case, we had only one choice. Sophia's parents had brothers and sisters in Israel who could send them an invitation, and upon arriving in Israel, they would be able to invite us. To leave Russia without us was a very hard decision for Sophia's parents. They were afraid that the Russians would not allow us to leave the country, and we would never see each other again. After long and difficult discussions, Sophia's parents finally agreed to do it. About a year and a half later, they left Russia and immediately sent invitations to both Sophia's brother and to us.

While waiting for the invitation, we were getting ready to apply. First, we had to obtain the blank forms from the KGB office responsible for immigration. This office created a rule that no more than ten applications per day would be issued. By doing that, they created a huge line of people who would have to register daily in order to not lose their spot. We registered the day Sophia's parents left Russia, and in doing so without invitation papers, we ran the risk of being identified as traitors. We could have faced huge problems, from being accused and thrown in jail to losing our jobs. In the end it worked out to our advantage. We got the applications within a month after receiving the invitation from Sophia's parents. It saved us at least three months, and in March of 1978 we began our process of fulfilling the necessary requirements in order to receive permission to leave Russia. On average, it took between one and two years to obtain all the paperwork and hear the decision made by the KGB.

The KGB's goal was to make this process as difficult as possible. Even though they hated Jews, the Russians didn't want to lose them. Most of the people who were trying to leave were well-educated, smart people. The officials discouraged people from applying by calling them traitors, making their employers fire them, kidnapping children, making false accusations, and putting applicants in jail. It was a very scary path, but we were determined to do it. From the moment we turned in our invitation to the KGB, we were publicly labeled "traitors" of the USSR, officially moving us to the category of second-class citizens. From that moment on, we had to be extra cautious with every step we took and watch every word we said. There were many known cases when the KGB would stage fights on the streets, get people who applied for exit visas involved, and arrest them. The arrest would immediately disqualify applicants from receiving the visas. There also were cases of kidnapping, and therefore we never walked alone on the streets; we walked only with other people, just in case we needed to have witnesses.

There were at least twenty release forms from different organizations we had to obtain before we were able to submit our official request to the KGB. The most difficult releases to obtain were the ones from the Komsomol party, Soviet army, and the housing authority. One of the biggest fears for everyone who applied was losing their job. In Russia, you couldn't be unemployed. You had to work to support your family, and without a source of income, the authorities could jail you. I knew that my managers liked my work and wouldn't want to lose me, but they had to convince the KGB person who was running the personnel department not to fire me. A lot of times managers were afraid to do that because they would then be viewed as sympathizers of the traitors and be demoted.

The day before I took the paperwork to the personnel department, I told two of my supervisors about my plans. Both of them told me that they would recommend for me to continue working, but they also told me that they couldn't control or guarantee the personnel department's decision. In the morning at the personnel department, I was expecting to hear that no traitors would be allowed to work there, and I would be asked to leave the building. To my surprise I was asked to leave the paperwork and go back to my office. Only later in the day did I realize that my direct boss was the reason I wasn't fired. He was a very nice and influential person, and he really liked my work. I was especially shocked because he was a communist trying to be promoted to the department manager. His favoritism toward me could tremendously reduce his chances in achieving this.

I ended up working as an engineer for the next two years, and that was huge. I was prepared, like the majority of engineers who applied to leave Russia, to do any unskilled work during this time. I worked very hard during this period, and my boss also made it clear to everyone that in the office, it would be business as usual, and none of my responsibilities would be taken away from me. We had quite a few conversations during those two years; he was trying to understand the reasons behind my decision to leave. Privately, he told me that he disagreed with the policies against Jews and hated to see us leaving the country.

On my last day of employment, with his permission, over forty people showed up in our office after work with a lot of food and drinks for a goodbye party. It was an almost unheard of event during the hard communist regime. After a few drinks most of them wished me luck and asked me to let them know how I was doing once I made it to Israel. None of this went over well with the communist and KGB bosses, and according to my Jewish friend who was working with me, my boss lost his bid to become the manager.

Immediately after informing the personnel department about my decision to apply for an exit visa, I had to inform the Komsomol boss of our company and ask to be dismissed from their organization. Komsomol—the youth pre-communist organization—was a place where the communists tried to brainwash young people. Without being a member of this organization, young people didn't have a chance to attend college. I'd had no choice but to join the organization at age fourteen. But since I wasn't interested in the communist party, I was a very passive member. All I did was pay my dues and attend mandatory meetings. Sophia and I stopped paying our dues and attending the meetings as soon as we made the decision to leave Russia. By doing that, we hoped to be expelled from the organization, but it didn't work, and we had to go through a humiliating process.

Since Komsomol was ruled and guided by the communist party, the process was created specifically to be very difficult. An open Komsomol meeting was held with at least 200 people in attendance, almost all of the employees being forced to attend. Among them were people who were sympathetic but afraid to show it, and people who really hated Jews would use this opportunity to show it publicly. This meeting was not only designed to humiliate people who asked to be expelled, but it was also intended to discourage other young Jewish people who were thinking of leaving Russia.

I was asked to come up to the podium and face those 200 angry people who just wanted to go home after work. When the Komsomol boss introduced me, he added that I was a "traitor of the Soviet Union." Everyone in the audience responded, screaming, "Shame to the traitors of the USSR." The screaming continued for a long time, and since communists were all around, everyone—even the sympathizers—had no choice but to participate. I was alone on the stage, and it was a pretty ugly and scary moment for me. Their goal was to scare me and try to get me to react verbally or even physically. I knew not to respond to any provocation because I would have been arrested and the visa process would have been postponed.

After the screaming part was over, the Komsomol boss asked the audience for volunteers who would like to come on stage to express their opinion regarding people like me. Prior to this meeting, the communist boss had selected a few people who were given written statements and told to read from them. All of the speeches were based on the same motive: to shame me, the traitor of the USSR. The speeches were designed to humiliate me and scare others who were considering doing what I was doing. They were trying to shame me for not being loyal to the country that had given me an education and where all citizens were equal. They were also trying to frighten me into thinking that, by going to a capitalist country, I would be treated as a second-class citizen because I wasn't born there.

After each speech, the audience again screamed, "Shame to the traitors." It was a very intimidating and unpleasant situation for me, but seeing some friends in the audience who were discreetly giving me the thumbs-up sign helped me keep my cool. I told myself that this would be over soon, and I made myself concentrate on the positive outcome. It worked well, and this process designed by communists to humiliate actually worked against them. In the end, I felt much better for having made the decision to leave all of that behind.

After the speeches and screaming were over, the Komsomol boss came to the stage to begin his part. He came very close to me and, in a manner intended to provoke me, began questioning me about my decision to emigrate. All of his questions were focused on the reason I had made the decision to leave Russia. I decided to use this opportunity to explain to everyone the real situation Jews were facing in Russia. As soon as communists in the audience understood what I was trying to do, they began to scream that I was a liar, and most of the people in the audience had no choice but to show their support and scream at me together with them. After the third unsuccessful attempt to explain my reasons, I decided to ignore all of their questions and asked for a vote to be expelled from the organization. Finally, two hours later, I was officially discharged from the Komsomol organization.

The next step was for the Kishinev's city Komsomol organization to hear me and agree with the company's decision to discharge me from the organization. I had to appear for a hearing in front of ten city Komsomol party members, who again used the opportunity to humiliate me and give me another scare over my decision to leave Russia. Usually this process took a few hours. In my case, I had a little help from the city's Komsomol boss, and without going through the usual routine I was officially discharged from the Komsomol organization of the USSR.

The reason for the break was that the city's Komsomol boss was a friend of mine—we graduated from college together and had spent a lot of time together studying and partying. Because his grandfather and father were communist bosses in other cities, he decided to follow in their footsteps and choose a political career. Within two years after graduation, he was appointed to lead the city's Komsomol party. Because of our close friendship, I knew that the public views he had to express differed from his personal views. We had kept in touch after graduation, and at a party at my house well before my public announcement, I had told him about my decision to leave. I wasn't surprised to hear that he understood and respected my decision.

After he had become the Komsomol boss we'd still kept in touch, though we were more careful—we had to make sure people wouldn't see us together in public, etc. During the city's Komsomol meeting he didn't allow others to question me, and all of his questions were related to the reason I had made this decision. After explaining my reason to the panel, he told everyone that there was nothing else to ask and made a motion to expel me from the organization. Sophia had to go through the same process I did. He helped make the process very easy by

21

choosing a time when only three of the city's members could attend, and within fifteen minutes Sophia was expelled from Komsomol. Shortly after both Sophia and I had been discharged from the organization, he came over for dinner. Sophia prepared the usual food, and after we had a few drinks, he told me that we had made the right decision to leave the USSR. He also told me that we wouldn't be able to communicate after my departure; however, he would check on us through our mutual friends. In addition, he asked for a big favor—a pair of Levi's jeans whenever we'd be able to afford it. It was very popular in Russia to wear American jeans, but the only place to buy them was the black market. The price was outrageous—200 rubles, while an average monthly engineering salary was half of that. I promised to send him a pair, and within a year I fulfilled my promise.

Chapter 4

Securing my discharge from the Soviet Army was the next big step for me. All male students attending Soviet colleges were given a military education during their college years. For the first four years of college, once a week, we had to dress in military uniforms and pretend that we were in the army. Upon graduation from college, we were sent for two months of training to the military. It was a reserve camp where the Russians kept their old equipment. My military training was in repair and maintenance of the artillery guns, and the only guns we ever touched were guns used during WWII; they never showed or let us work on the new equipment. However, from the moment I asked to be discharged, everything changed, and the Soviet army officials began treating me like an officer who had high security clearance.

I was called to appear in front of a special military committee that did the same thing as the Komsomol members had done. For almost two hours, high-ranking military officers screamed at me, trying to scare me. This was very different and much more serious than the Komsomol process. If the military committee had ruled that my knowledge and involvement with the army was a threat to national security, I would have been denied the exit visa, and for the next three years I wouldn't have been allowed to apply again. During the meeting, some of the senior officers tried to scare me by saying that the KGB had very long arms all over the world, and should I share my knowledge with the CIA, they would find and kill me. Another officer told me that my parents and sister would be jailed if I talked to foreign intelligences.

Suddenly, one of the officers approached me and, still screaming, asked me to identify the names of my foreign connections in Israel or the USA and the amount of money I had been promised in exchange for information about the Russian military. I knew that I couldn't get into an argument, so my answers were very short, no matter how hard they tried to provoke me. There was also a KGB officer at this meeting who was taking notes and being quiet most of the time. At the end of the meeting, before the decision was made, he gave me a big scare by making a comment regarding my parents' safety, assuring me that they would be punished if I talked to the CIA or other intelligence services.

Finally, after grilling me for over two hours, I was told to wait in the waiting room. Behind the closed doors a group of military people, whose job it was to make any Jewish person's life as miserable as possible, was making a decision that would affect my family's future. My knowledge of the military wasn't significant, nor was it important, but I knew that nobody would question their decision, should they decide to keep me in the USSR. Until I was discharged from the army, I wouldn't have a chance to complete my application and leave the Soviet Union.

It took them about an hour before they called me in. I was very nervous and had no idea what to expect. Without making any comments, the chief officer told me to hand him my military ID, and he stamped it "DISCHARGED." He then signed the application I was carrying, officially acknowledging that I was discharged from the Soviet army and that the army was allowing me to leave the USSR. He made me sign a paper stating that should I not receive permission to leave the country, I would never be reinstated as an officer and would have to serve as a private in the event that I had to serve in the army.

What a relief that was! It was the most important step so far in our process, and finally we saw a light at the end of the tunnel. The last signature we had to obtain was the signature from the housing committee stating that our condo had been returned to the government in good shape. Even though it was our private condo that we had paid for in full, we couldn't sell it. The only choice we had was to give it away to the government. Instead of making money from the sale, we had to pay the contractors to bring the apartment to perfect condition. Like everything else, the government made this process as difficult as possible. To meet the requirements, we had to vacate our condo until contractors could return it to its original condition. After all repairs had been made, a special committee had to accept the condo. There were five people on the acceptance committee, and as a rule, after the initial visit each of them would find a few items to be fixed. The next time, they would find more problems we had to fix. It was common to try at least three times before they would accept the apartment. We had to move everything out, so we moved in with Sophia's brother, Sam, who didn't have to go through this process because he was living in his parent-in-laws' house.

Finally, after all the problems identified by the committee were fixed, I was in their office to arrange for the final inspection. Suddenly one of the committee members approached me with a message that a telephone call from the KGB had just been received requesting that I, together with my wife, show up in two hours at their headquarters. He also told me that the committee had been instructed not to accept our apartment until the KGB cleared up this matter.

I had a terrible feeling about this, and on the way home I stopped at the telephone station and called my parents to let them know, so they would be able to track us if the KGB locked us up. Sam and his wife, Janet, were also called to show up at the KGB. All four of us met in front of the headquarters building. We were very concerned, not knowing what to expect. There were two officers waiting for us in the KGB lobby. They asked us to follow them, and each of us was placed in a different room. It was very scary when they told me to go into a room while they took Sophia away; we had no idea why we were there or if we'd see each other again.

The room was small and dark with a table and chair. As soon as I sat down, a very bright light hit my face. There was no way to escape the light, and it was very intimidating. An officer came into the room and immediately began questioning me about my reasons for wanting to leave Russia. When I tried to ask his reason for questioning me after we had received their permission to leave, I got a very straightforward answer: "This is not the place for you to ask questions." Suddenly, the officer who was behind me turned my chair around and screamed in my face, asking for the name of the person we had bribed to get permission to leave Russia.

It took me a few seconds to understand his question and what exactly he was trying to get from me. After telling him that I had no idea what he was talking about, he pulled a piece of paper from the desk and began trying to intimidate me by pushing it into my face. He told me that this was an anonymous letter the KGB had received from a citizen. The letter supposedly had some information that both my brother-in-law and I had bribed a KGB official in order to get our exit permissions. With a smile, he told me that as soon as I gave him the name, my family would be allowed to leave Russia; otherwise, we'd all be kept in Russia. He told me to wait in the room and that I'd better have an answer when he returned.

I was trapped there, not knowing where Sophia was or what would happen next. Suddenly the room lights went on, the door opened, and the officer entered the room, telling me that it was all over, and as soon as I confirmed the answers my wife had given them, we'd be free to go. He was bluffing, of course, and became very angry when I repeated my answers. He left the room again, and on the way out threatened to lock me up until they got an answer from me. He also told me that since my wife was talking, they'd let her go without seeing me.

Looking back on this time, I think it was probably one of the most terrifying moments in my life, sitting in a small, dark room at the KGB headquarters, feeling helpless, not knowing if I'd ever see Sophia, Robby, my sister, or my parents again. I was left alone for about thirty minutes. When the door opened, another officer came into the room and told me to follow him. We entered a large room, and I saw Janet there. When the officer left, she told me what had happened to her, and it was exactly what I'd experienced. We were trying to understand why just two of us were in the room and where Sophia and Sam were. Finally, the door opened and Sophia was escorted into the room. It was a very special moment in our lives. After almost half a day of not knowing each other's whereabouts, we were together.

Sophia's story was the same as mine: the officer had asked her to confirm the names of the officials I had provided them. It took another thirty minutes until Sam showed up, and finally we were all together.

We knew that the room was wired, and only when we were all together again did we felt more comfortable. We decided that talking loudly could benefit our situation. Knowing that the officers were listening and taping our conversation, we began a loud discussion of what to do if any of us were kept in jail. We were also discussing what to do in case the KGB revoked our permission to leave Russia, and we agreed that we would go to Moscow, try to get in touch with the US Consulate, and maybe with the International Olympic Committee as well, because the Olympic Games in Moscow were coming up in the summer of 1980. Our goal was to let the KGB know that we would not be quiet, and hopefully they would let us go.

When two officers entered the room, I was almost certain that they would separate us again. Instead, they sat down and began asking us the same questions again. After receiving no answers from us, they again reminded us that we would not be allowed to leave Russia until this issue was resolved. When we asked what happened to the permission we had already received, the officer told us with a big smile on his face that the KGB would let us know when and if we'd be allowed to leave the country. The officer also told us that our case was very low priority to them, and his recommendation for us to receive an update was to contact the KGB not earlier than a month from now. Of course, we could call them any time with the information they were looking for. Shortly thereafter, we were told that we were free to go.

Even though we had received terrible news about our status being revoked, at that moment we were all very happy because nobody was being arrested, and all of us would leave the KGB headquarters together.

Chapter 5

Another problem arose: Sophia and I suddenly realized that we didn't have a place to live—our apartment was empty. Also, since our work permits, diplomas, and passports had been taken away from us, we couldn't get jobs or drive cars. And we had no choice but to move into my parents' apartment in Beltsy. According to the USSR's standards, my parents had a good-sized apartment: two bedrooms, a living room, and a kitchen, all about 800 square feet. My parents were happy to spend time together with us, but none of us were able to truly enjoy it due to our uncertainty about our future. About two weeks later, I decided to go back to Kishinev and try to get in touch with the deputy interior minister of our state, a two-star general who was in charge of the investigating department.

Upon my arrival, I was told that there were only two days each month that the general would see people, and it was between the hours of eight and eleven a.m. I was also told that there were no appointments; it worked on a first-come, first-served basis. In other words, I had to come very early and stay in line until they opened the doors. If the general was in a good mood, he would see the first twenty people in line, but there were days when he would see only ten people. The first opportunity I had was about a week later. The night before, I drove to Kishinev so both Sam and I could be at the KGB office by around two a.m. in order to be one of the first ten people in line. At that time, there were already six people in front of us. Knowing that the first ten in line usually had a chance to see the general, we didn't mind spending the night, staying in line. By eight a.m., there were about forty people waiting to see him.

Nobody would leave until the last person seen by the general updated everyone.

All of us had a common issue—trying to leave the USSR—and we all wanted to know the latest developments. Before we were allowed to see the general, his staff interviewed us. In addition to learning about our case, they were also trying to determine what questions we planned to ask the general.

My name was called, and I was escorted to general's office. Without looking up, he asked me if I finally had an answer to their question. Immediately upon hearing my answer, he ordered the guards to escort me out of his office. They didn't let me ask him any questions. As I was leaving, he advised me not to come back until I had the names they were looking for and told me that nothing would be done on his part without this information.

It would be two weeks from this date before the general would see people again, and both Sam and I decided to come back. We were extra careful because it would have been a perfect time for the KGB to fabricate incidents against us, in which case we would be jailed. Most of our time was spent inside my parents' apartment, studying English. It was my first introduction to the English language. French was the foreign language I had studied at school and college. For Sophia, it was a different story. She had studied English in school and college and was pretty good at it, even winning state competitions. Sophia gets all of the credit for teaching me English, and because of her, I could actually understand some English when we arrived in America.

Two weeks passed, and I was back in Kishinev to see the general. It was a repeat of my previous visit; no changes or progress had been made. The KGB wouldn't let us leave the country; our request to reverse their permission was declined, so we ended up in a terrible situation without any legal rights. We couldn't work and had to remain with my parents. Time was passing, and we realized that without doing something drastic, we would have no chance to exit.

We came up with a plan to go to Moscow, try to get in touch with the American Consulate, and ask for help. Moscow at that time was getting ready for the Olympic Games; there were a lot of foreigners, and we hoped to be able to pass our information to one of them to forward it to the Americans. It was a very difficult and dangerous plan. We had no chance of getting into the American Embassy; Russians did not allow ordinary people to go to any embassy in Moscow, and we didn't have any justification for being there. The KGB closely watched each foreigner in Russia, and the majority wouldn't even talk to the Russian people on the streets. The hotels where the foreigners stayed were off limits to Russians, so our plan was to try, and hope that some of the foreigners would be willing to take the risk and help us. We would also have ended up in a KGB prison if we had been caught talking to foreigners. We knew it would be a challenge, and to make sure that whoever might be willing to accept the risk and take our papers would understand our request, we wrote our story in English.

Next, we had to let the general know about our plans, which was a very dangerous move for us, because we would be advising him of our willingness to go against him, demanding a quick solution to our situation. It had been almost three months since the beginning of our ordeal. We also decided to bluff and tell the general that we had friends in Moscow who already had our information and who would forward it to the US authorities if we did not contact them within a week.

During our next appointment, after the general's talk I knew that this was the moment to speak. I began to talk, and for the initial few seconds I felt like I was going to faint. My feet were shaking, and sweat was covering my body and face. It was probably one of the tensest moments in my life, as I knew he could either lock me up or let me go to the free world. I made myself concentrate on my voice because it was very important for him to see that I was not afraid, that everything I was telling him was already in place and would be executed if I were not allowed to leave the building, or if we were again denied permission to leave. I remember well how the general's smiling face became very nasty.

The colonel standing behind the general moved toward me, screaming that I'd be going to prison instead of Israel. It was very hard, but somehow I controlled my emotions and didn't show them that I was afraid. Finally, the general ordered the guard to escort me to the waiting room and not allow me to leave the building. Sam was next to see the general, and I had a chance to tell him that I did everything we planned to do. After he was escorted from the general's office, both of us sat and waited, very scared. It was over an hour after the general had seen the last person when two guards appeared and ordered Sam and me to follow them to the general's office. I was so sure the general was going to tell us that we were going to prison; it took a moment for me to realize that he was saying something else. Without even looking in our direction, he told us that he had made a decision and that the decision was strictly based on his conversation with our investigator, and not on the fact that we were threatening him with our Moscow plans. He told us that he would allow us to leave Russia.

It was a moment in my life I'll never forget. Even now, thirty-five years later, I can remember every second. Sam and I just realized that we were free to leave Russia. WOW, what a feeling it was! The general ordered us to prepare our papers so we would be able to finish the paperwork process before leaving the country. It was like a dream I didn't want to end, and I realized that I didn't hear or see what was going on around me when Sam asked me about our departure time, and everyone in the room was waiting to hear my answer. They wanted to know if we could leave Russia within three months.

Like everything else, the departure process was made very difficult, and once you committed to a date, you couldn't miss it. Under normal circumstances, three months would have been a sufficient amount of time; however, in our situation we were afraid that the KGB would change the decision again. I knew that my dad's connections with the railroad company would help to expedite the most important and difficult task, which would be obtaining tickets from Kishinev to Vienna. It was common knowledge that without connections and bribes, sometimes even three months was not a sufficient time to obtain them. With that in mind, and with the fear of being held again for other reasons, I told the general that we'd be out of the country within one month. I also knew that by expediting our departure, our time together with my parents would be shortened, but at the same time, no matter how difficult it would be for him, my dad would never say no to my request. I made the phone call to him after leaving the KGB office, and by the time I made it back to Beltsy, he had already made the arrangements for our luggage to be checked by Customs. Most impressive was that the ticket reservations from Kishinev to Vienna for all of us were made within a few days.

My parents' apartment was a very emotional place. Sophia and I were very happy that we would finally be on

33

our way, and my parents and sister were thrilled for us but very sad that we would soon be separated. At the same time, we all were quite uneasy, not knowing what challenges awaited us or when we'd be able to be together again. We also knew that we had to accomplish a lot in a very short timeframe. My dad took the leadership role in guiding us through. He used all of his connections to make sure that there would be no problems in meeting our departure date. He never told me the amount of money he spent, but my estimate was that he probably spent at least five years' salary to make everything go smoothly.

We were allowed to ship 500 lbs. of personal belongings. We had it stored at Sam's house, where we also had a large wooden container to ship our stuff. Since officially we were going to Israel, our container had to be shipped via sea to Israel and then shipped to America. When we delivered the container to Customs, it was opened and every item was inspected. While checking the items, they also decided what to let go and what was illegal to take out of the country.

Some of the items we packed we never used. For example, since there was a big shortage of toilet paper in Russia, we decided to take a lot of it with us. We never used it because by the time we received our box—nine months after our arrival—we wondered how in the world something that rough and scratchy could be used, and all of it went into the garbage. The same happened to thirty boxes of Russian cigarettes. When we tried them they were so stinky, we threw them away. However, we had also packed items that did help us, such as sets of goose down pillows, sheets, and towels, all of which we used.

Again, because my dad didn't want to take any chances, he came with us, found the person who was in charge during this shift, and gave him a sizable bribe. It worked well; our box was opened just for a few minutes, the supervisor ordered it closed after we cut out the dates on the photos, and it was on its way to Israel.

Back in Kishinev we had to finish the last task, which was to give our condo to the government. We were so afraid of something going wrong that, for a whole day, Sophia and I cleaned our empty place even though it had been ready four months earlier. Again, my dad decided not to take any chances and bribed the chief inspector as soon as he walked into our empty condo. Because of that, the inspection went very smoothly, and within an hour all of the necessary papers were signed.

The following morning, we delivered our papers to the KGB office—the same KGB building where the general's office was. We felt very uncomfortable going into the building, and even more uncomfortable leaving all the signed papers with the secretary without getting any receipt. At that time, it was impossible to make photocopies in Russia, so we had no proof of having turned in all of our signed papers. Upon leaving our papers, we were told to come back two days later to get our visas. The final signature in order to obtain the visas was the general's signature, and yes, we were afraid that he would retaliate against us, but we had no choice.

Immediately upon leaving the KGB office, we went to my brother-in-law and spent the next two days inside his house; we had no documents, no legal rights, and were afraid of any staged KGB provocation. After spending two days at Sam's house, all of us, including the small children, showed up at the KGB office, where we had to wait for hours before we were asked to pay 600 rubles for each adult in order to renounce our Russian citizenship. Only after we paid them were we given our exit visas.

It was a great moment. After two and a half years of hell, we finally held in our hands the papers to our freedom! At that time, it was the biggest achievement of our lives.

Chapter 6

Our triumphant moment was overwhelming and wonderful, but we had no time to celebrate. Since we would be traveling through Czechoslovakia and Austria, we had to obtain permission from both to enter their countries. Every adult had to appear in person at both embassies in Moscow, and we had to do it fast. In order to get tickets to Moscow, we had to bribe the airline employees. After we paid triple the price for the tickets, we got the tickets and arrived in Moscow a few days later.

In Moscow, we had to obtain entry visas to both Czechoslovakia and Austria. We asked Sophia's cousin, a student at Moscow's university, to keep a place in line at the Czech embassy for us while we went to the Austrian embassy. By doing this, we were able to get to both embassies in one day, and finally it was time for us to celebrate. By selling our car, furniture, and everything we owned, we made a good amount of money and still had a lot left by the time we went to Moscow.

We also knew that we would only be allowed 300 rubles per visa to exchange for US dollars. We decided to spend some of the money at a good Moscow restaurant. Together with Sophia's cousin and her second cousin, we ended up at the most exclusive restaurant in Moscow, the Slavyansky Bazar. One of the restaurant's highlights was the bottom floor; it was a large pond with fish. Customers could catch their own fish, and it would be prepared for you. When we entered the restaurant we made sure the staff knew we had money to spend. We ended up in a private room, and when the waiter showed up, we asked him to bring everything offered on the menu. We spent over six hours and more than 1,000 rubles there (almost nine months' engineering salary), and it was our farewell to Russian food and culture.

The next day we were back in Kishinev, and a group of our friends—who weren't afraid of having us as their friends—threw a party for us. Some people who were in the process of obtaining their visas just showed up to hear our experience and get tips, while others came to wish us the best and say goodbye.

The next day we went back to Beltsy. I wanted to spend as much time as possible with my parents and sister. There was only one week left before our departure, and we spent it together. It was a very emotional time for both my parents and me because we knew that this would be the last time we could be together.

At that time my biggest concern was my dad's health. Since 1961 he'd had kidney problems, and his health was rapidly deteriorating. He had to be on dialysis, but in the USSR at that time, dialysis was only available at Moscow's government hospital. My mom's health wasn't good either, and our departure didn't help either of them.

Only years later, when our kids were grown, were we able to fully understand what it meant and how they must have felt to let us go, especially with us leaving to go to another country. While at my parents', every night we went to bed very late, talking and listening to their advice. To spend more time with my dad, I went to work with him, and only then did he tell me how he had made the extra money so his family would not struggle but would have a comfortable life. My dad's official salary was about 150 rubles per month, which wouldn't even cover the rent, utilities, and groceries. This was very typical for most Russian families, and most people tried to make extra money. Since free enterprise was forbidden, anything people did to earn extra money was considered illegal, and a lot of people ended up in prison for doing this.

Russians had a special police force hunting people like my dad, who wanted their families to have a decent life. However, most of the officials' salaries, including the special police personnel, were also not sufficient to provide a comfortable living situation for their families. Since most of them were also interested in providing well for their loved ones, they were open to accepting bribes from people they trusted. By doing that they would close their eyes, allowing my dad and people like him to make extra money. My dad never talked to me in detail about what he was doing. He didn't want me to worry, nor did he want me to learn this kind of business, just in case it would influence me to do the same in order to provide a better life for my own family. The details I learned from my dad during this last week made me really proud of him. All the extra money he made came from good deeds he did for other families. All I learned about him in the final week only added to the stories I'd heard from everyone about my dad. He was a very kind and very giving person.

Throughout our final week in Russia, my mom tried very hard to keep her emotions in check and not show how difficult it was for her to let us go. She did well until the last day. All day long she was crying, hugging all of us, and wouldn't let Robby out of her sight. Emotions ran very high, and a few times I cried together with her. My Aunt Fania, Dad's oldest sister, was also taking our exit very hard because we were so close. As I was talking to her and her husband, Uncle Youil, he asked me to follow him to the kitchen. There he told me that he would like to teach me how to make a very inexpensive and easy-to-prepare meal. The meal was the traditional Moldavian-Jewish meal called mamaliga (very similar to polenta), with the main components being cornmeal and water. The reason for teaching me how to make it, he said, was because it had helped them a lot during WWII, and also when they didn't have enough money to buy better food. The preparation of this meal was very simple: bring the salty water to a boil in an iron pot, add the corn meal while mixing it constantly with a wooden stick. In less than ten minutes, I prepared a very inexpensive and quite tasty meal. Before my mom arrived in America, I made mamaliga only a few times. After she arrived and brought the original iron pot and wooden stick, I made it quite often. When I made it the first time for my mom, she requested it at least once a month thereafter, and I knew that I had mastered it.

It was well after midnight when people who had come to say goodbye began hugging Sophia and me, most of them realizing that this would probably be the last time they would ever see us, and it was very hard. In the morning, together with my parents, Polina, and Aunt Fania, we left for Kishinev.

Our train was leaving the next day at four p.m. on the first leg from Kishinev to Chop, the border city with Czechoslovakia. My sister and Sam's best friend decided to come with us to Chop; they wanted to spend more time with us and also wanted to be there to collect any items Customs might not allow us to take. As it had happened in Beltsy, a lot of people came to Sam's house to say goodbye; for most of them it was the last time they would ever see us. In the morning when I woke up, realizing that in a few hours I'd be leaving my parents behind, I suddenly became so nervous that I had to leave the house. Without realizing what I was doing, I found myself at the barbershop talking to the hairdresser I used for the last few years. After my hair was done I let him know that this was the last haircut for me, and the reason behind it. To my surprise he became very emotional. He didn't want to take any money from me and wished me all the best. As I was leaving he hugged me, telling me that he was jealous.

There were at least thirty people who showed up at the railroad station. Everyone was trying to talk to us, giving us some last-minute advice, hugging and kissing us. My parents, with Robby in their arms, wouldn't let me out of their sight. Emotions were very high; all we were doing was looking at each other, holding hands, and crying. My dad couldn't hide his feelings anymore and was doing something I'd never seen: he was openly crying. Both of us also knew that, because of his poor health, this could be the last time we would see each other. I was trying to comfort him by talking about our future together in America. Dad and Mom were telling us that even though they were very scared and upset about losing us, they were happy for us that we decided to take this opportunity to improve our lives. I felt so bad leaving them behind in Russia, however I was hopeful that within a year and a half we could be together again because I knew they would apply for visas within six months. I was also thinking that based on our immigration experience, we would be able to make their lives much easier upon their arrival in America. Those thoughts made me feel better and helped during this tough time.

Finally, it was time to board the train. Everyone was hugging us and saying goodbye. I couldn't take my eyes off my parents—my mom and dad were still crying. I couldn't help it, tears were flowing from my eyes. My mom had a very hard time, so my cousin and my aunt were holding her. After she hugged and kissed Sophia and Robby, I approached her, and she began to cry even harder. I knew that my goodbye had to be a short one because she could faint. My dad was next to me at all times and was trying to calm her down, but she wouldn't let me go. My dad made a very smart move—he asked Robby to hug his grandmother again. That made her switch her attention, and she let me go.

Then it was my dad's turn to say goodbye. To make it easier on both of us, for the first time he told me that he was sure we'd see each other soon. He told me to be aware of anything seeming and looking too good to be true, because it could be a trap. And even though I've heard it many times here in America, my dad was the first to tell me this. I acted on this advice at all times and still do.

Lastly, he asked me to do everything in my power to bring my sister to America so we could be together, should he or Mom not be around anymore. Family was the most important issue for my parents, and I promised my dad that nothing would stop me from keeping my promise. He also told me how proud he was that I had the courage to leave Russia for a better future and hopefully make a better future for our entire family. My dad had a lot of faith in the Jewish organizations, and he told me not to be afraid to contact them and ask for help if needed. He was the first one who told me about the B'nai B'rith Organization.

As he was telling me all of this, the train started to move. We hugged for a few seconds, and when I jumped up to the steps, my dad wouldn't let my hand go. As the train moved faster, he walked faster and faster, looking directly in my eyes, tears streaming from my eyes and his, and then came the moment when he had to let my hand go. Even now, I can clearly see the look on my dad's face. I'll never be able to forget that moment of my life; it was definitely one of the hardest I ever had.

I never saw my dad again.

Last day in Kishinev
Sam, Polina, Mom, Dad, Cousin Issak
Sophia, Robby, me, Aunt Fania

Chapter 7

The train ride to Chop was around ten hours. We arrived early in the morning, and our train to Bratislava was scheduled to leave around seven p.m. During most of the ride to Chop, I spent time talking to my sister. We were working on the strategies of applying different codes to our letters and telephone conversations so the KGB would not understand the real meanings of our correspondences. I told her about Dad's request and my promise for us to be together, and we assured each other that we'd make it happen. Her husband, who overheard our conversation, again assured me that in six months they would start the visa process. He also promised that he would take care of my parents the same way he would his own parents, which made me feel better.

Upon arriving in Chop and completing the necessary paperwork, we waited for Customs to clear our luggage. When they called our names, it was time for us to say goodbye to everyone. Once we entered the room where the luggage was checked, we wouldn't be allowed to come back. Again, as it was in Kishinev, it was very difficult to say goodbye to my sister. We both cried, but we knew that sooner or later we'd be together again. Robby had developed a very strong bond with Polina, especially during the preceding four months, and he didn't want to let her go—we had to pull him away from her.

When we entered the room we knew that Sam and his family were next in line. We were hoping that all of us would be called together, but the Customs officers didn't allow them to come in with us. The large room was divided in half by a white line. In addition to the regular Customs officers, there were at least ten KGB officers in the room.

44

KGB officers looked straight into our eyes while the Customs officers checked our belongings, and it made us very uncomfortable. All we were allowed was one piece of luggage per person.

In the suitcases, together with necessary personal belongings, we had packed items such as photo equipment and some mechanical tools. It was done based on the information from people who had left Russia before us. According to them, the sales money from the photo and mechanical items would get us through the stay in Italy. However, all those extras made our suitcases very large and heavy.

My dad was really good at packing; he had done a great job packing our personal belongings together with the items we took for sale. Sophia was carrying one suitcase, and I had two, one of them extremely large. We also hung on Robby's chest a large photo camera and a pair of binoculars.

After our suitcases went through the X-ray machine, we were ordered to remove all the items from the suitcases. When they were empty, the officers used sharp probes to check that nothing was hidden in the suitcase walls. Next, they hand-checked each item, and if they decided it was okay for us to take it with us, they would throw it on the floor. We were not allowed to pick up anything until they had checked everything, so pretty soon there was a big mess on the floor. The officers were enjoying this process and laughing, and all we could do was watch.

When the tools were pulled out, they questioned me as to why we had them in the carry-on luggage. If I had told them the truth, they would have had a good enough reason to confiscate them. I answered that I was a mechanical engineer, and until I found an engineering job, I was planning to use the tools for rebuilding engines in order to make a living. To make sure I was telling the truth, they asked questions about individual tools and how I would use each of them. I knew what the tools were for and correctly answered all of their questions. Only then were the tools allowed to go, so they ended up on the floor with our other possessions.

Next, they asked why we had so many pieces of photo equipment. After answering that we were planning to use it in the future for our own use and that we didn't know when we'd be able to purchase new photo equipment, the Customs officers couldn't find a reason for not allowing us to take it. The photo equipment also ended up on the floor. After all of our belongings had been removed from the suitcases and dropped to the floor, the officers found that some of the photos we had with us had handwritten dates on the back.

Because the Russians were afraid that any information would jeopardize their security, we had to cut out the dates from the photos so we would be allowed to take them with us. We still have those photos with cut off corners. We also had a few books with us but weren't allowed to take them. The Russians had a rule that any book printed before 1976 was considered a national treasure, and the books we had were printed prior to that date.

Next they checked our jewelry. Each adult was allowed to take four pieces, weighing not more than five grams each. In addition to the weight, the officers also were deciding whether any of the jewelry items would be considered a national treasure. All I had in addition to my wedding ring was another small ring, so they had no problems with me. Sophia, in addition to her wedding ring, had three more pieces. The officers decided that two pieces of her jewelry fell into the national treasure category and let her take only one. The officers were the only authorities in the room, and there was no one to whom we could appeal; their decision was final.

My sister was waiting outside the room and collected everything we weren't allowed to take with us. After checking our belongings, it was time for the personal search before they would allow us to board the train. First we were asked to remove our coats. While our coats were searched, the officers made sure we had nothing hidden under our clothes. They even asked me to remove my shoes and sent them through an X-ray machine. The worst part was when they undressed Robby all the way to his underwear. He was crying, but neither Sophia nor I were allowed to comfort him. I felt so helpless, I couldn't help my son who was crying and asking for help. They did it because they were afraid that we might use a little child to smuggle items such as important papers, pictures, jewelry, etc. out of the country. When they found nothing on him, Sophia was finally allowed to dress Robby.

By the time all searches were completed, we had less than an hour left before our train's departure. We were told to hurry up and pack our suitcases; we had to be on the train thirty minutes prior to its departure. There was no way for us to repack our suitcases that fast. We filled them up the best we could, and whatever items we couldn't fit, we carried in our hands to the train. Only when we were on the way to the train did we realize that Sam wasn't even in the search room, so there was no chance of him making it to this train.

Suddenly, even before we left Russia, we were facing a very difficult task by leaving the country all by ourselves without anyone we could count on. We also didn't know where and how we would be able to meet Sam. It was a very scary situation for us. When we asked one of the officers if it was possible for Sam to make it to this train, he answered with a smile that he had no chance of making it. We even asked if there was a possibility for us to wait until the next day so we could leave together. Keeping the smile on his face, he told us that the only way for us to proceed was to the train, which was leaving in thirty minutes. They didn't even allow us to talk to Sam, so we couldn't make any arrangements to meet in Vienna.

Again, the communists did what they did best: caused as many troubles as possible for the Jews leaving their country. The officers who escorted us made us walk very fast, and every time we would stop for a break they got angry and screamed at us to hurry up. When Robby started to cry, one of the officers told us that the traitors to the USSR deserved this treatment.

By the time we reached the train, about 300 yards away from the search room, I was very tired and wanted to take a break before loading the suitcases. Sophia and Robby stepped inside the train, and I was preparing to load the suitcases one at a time. The conductor began screaming that I had no time to carry them one at a time—we had to bring them all together. Sophia had to come down the steps to carry a very heavy suitcase while I was pulling two at the same time. Robby had a lot of stuff hanging on him. He was crying, but we didn't have a chance to stop and comfort him or take a break—our conductor kept screaming and hurrying us. I was ready to kick him in his smiling face, but I knew better than that; I had to control myself.

Almost all of the compartments were empty, but the conductor made us go all the way to the end and directed us to a compartment with two women in it. He also told me that he would not leave the compartment until I stored all of our luggage. Under the lower seat there was only one available space, so I had no choice but to place two large suitcases at the third level, about six and a half feet above the floor. I had no problem placing the first one there, but when I tried to place the second, which weighed about eighty pounds, I couldn't do it. Then when I saw the conductor's smiling face, Sophia's scared face, and heard Robby crying, I knew I had no choice but to do it. I sat down, picked up the suitcase, placed it on my head, slowly stood up, and from my head moved it up to the third level. Even today when I think about that situation, I don't know how I did it.

After the suitcases were finally in place, I was able to help Sophia and Robby, who were still holding a lot of things in their hands that we couldn't fit in the suitcases. We had to place them back in the suitcases, but because I couldn't reach the heavy suitcase on the top, we had to work with only two of the suitcases. And we were trying to do all that without disturbing the two women in our compartment. Somehow we did it, and by the time we pulled away from the station our suitcases were closed and put away. As we began moving away, Robby became very thirsty, and we looked for some water. When I asked our conductor for a glass of water, he told me that in Israel they have good water, and Robby would have to wait and get it there. We felt helpless; our child wanted a drink and was crying and asking for water, and there was nothing we could do to help him. Finally, one of the women in our compartment decided to help us. They knew that we were Jewish and leaving for Israel and were not very sympathetic to us. But after seeing the conductor's behavior, one of them stepped out and returned shortly with a glass of water. It was a great relief, and after finishing his drink, Robby fell asleep.

About an hour after leaving Chop, we crossed the border of Czechoslovakia. At the first stop, both women got off the

49

train, and we were left alone in the compartment. It would have been a perfect time for us to get some sleep, but there were no sheets, pillows, or blankets. However, when repacking, I had come across three bottles of vodka we were allowed to take with us. With a bottle of vodka in my hands, I approached our conductor and asked if it was possible to get some pillows and blankets. It worked; he took the bottle, told me to go back, and showed up soon after with pillows and sheets for all of us. He also brought a bottle of water and glasses. When I thanked him, he explained the reason he'd been mean. If he had shown any sympathy toward us, he could lose his job. Keeping this job was very important to him because going to Czechoslovakia on regular basis allowed him to buy items that were hard to get in Russia and sell them for a big profit.

Soon we were left alone in the compartment when suddenly Sophia started to cry. I had never seen her crying like that. She was shivering, she couldn't talk to me, and it looked like she was having an anxiety attack. After a couple of very hard days, after going through Customs and now not knowing when she'd meet her brother, Sophia broke down. We weren't allowed to take any medicine with us, so there was nothing I could use to calm her down. I grabbed a pack of cigarettes, ran to the conductor and exchanged it for a hot glass of tea. Hot tea worked, and after drinking a couple of glasses she fell asleep. Watching them both asleep, I began to realize how huge of a responsibility both Sophia and I suddenly acquired. It was just the two of us, without any backup, without people who could advise us like parents or friends. I also realized that from here on, every time different situations would arise, they would have to be resolved only by two of us, and the fact that we were separated from Sam and his family didn't help.

While Sophia and Robby were asleep, I repacked all of our suitcases. The bottle of vodka and cigarettes went a long way; as we approached Bratislava, our conductor again brought us hot water and tea. Sophia and I had hot tea, and we used the hot water to make some food for Robby. Soon it was time to remove the suitcase from the top shelf, and I couldn't understand how in the world I had been able to place it there. Again I had to use my head as a support to lower it to the floor. It was pretty challenging, but it was much easier than putting it up there. When the train stopped, our conductor allowed me to take out one suitcase at a time, and that helped a lot. Sophia and Robby were waiting outside, and I took my time unloading the suitcases. It was around eight a.m. when we arrived in Bratislava; our train to Vienna was leaving at four p.m. from another track about 400 yards away.

As we were trying to figure out how we were going to move our suitcases, we spotted another group of people about thirty yards away. They looked very similar to us, uncertain where to go, and also had a lot of luggage. I approached them and asked if they spoke Russian, realizing right away that we were going to the same place. That was a huge relief for both of us. The group we met was a family of two young couples with two children, along with a mother and a father for each of the couples. They were from Chernovtsy, not too far from Beltsy. There was another couple, also going to America, and they were from Tashkent.

Together we moved our suitcases close to theirs. It was such a relief for me because Sophia and Robby would not be left alone while I checked where to go and what to do next. I learned that we had to move to the railroad station and wait there until our train to Vienna arrived. As I was walking back to our families I found an empty cart and was very happy because by using the cart, I would be able to move all of the suitcases together. The other couple spotted another empty cart and went to pick it up. As I was pushing the empty cart back to where Sophia was waiting, I suddenly felt something cold touching my forehead. I stopped and looked up. What I saw was a policeman pointing his gun at my head. That was terrifying, I had no idea why I had been stopped.

I was afraid to make any movement and took my hands off the cart. I knew that no matter what the policeman did next, I had to keep cool and follow all of his commands. It was known that the Czechoslovakians didn't like Jews and would do everything in their power to make our lives miserable while we were passing through their country. I had no idea what he was telling me. The only word I understood was the word "GID", the same slang word Russians called Jews. Finally, thanks to an elderly woman who stopped and explained that I was not allowed to use the cart, the situation calmed down. As I was standing and waiting for the others to return, the policeman started laughing at me, and in perfect Russian told me that we, the Jews, deserved this kind of treatment from his country because in addition to being Jewish we were also traitors of the communist regime. Finally, after a few trips, we brought all of our luggage to the railroad station.

Robby and the other couples' small children were getting hungry. Since we didn't have any local currency, I decided to trade some of the cigarettes we were allowed to take with us for money. I took two packs of Marlboro, went outside the station, and was able to explain to the people who stopped that I needed money to feed three small children. A few people didn't want to listen, but there was a man who pulled the money out his pocket and even walked me to the place where we could buy milk, bread, and cheese. The amount of the money I got was enough to buy food and feed our children two times. None of the adults felt hungry, all we wanted at that time was to leave the communist country as soon as possible.

In the afternoon, we were told to move our luggage to the tracks where our train was already parked. By then we knew better than to look for carts. All of the train doors were closed, and the policemen were present to make sure we didn't open them. They were trying to intimidate us, talking and laughing at us, but we also knew to ignore them. We had only a few more hours to deal with the communists, and that was very encouraging for us. The doors were opened fifteen minutes before the departure time, and as it happened back in Russia, we were told to load our luggage very quickly. Using the last opportunity to show their hatred of us, the policemen were screaming and telling us to move the suitcases back to the compartments as quickly as possible. This time, however, because there were four men, we all helped each other, moved our luggage very quickly, and within five minutes everyone was situated in their compartments. Shortly thereafter, all doors were locked, and the train departed.

Fifteen minutes later the train stopped, and the Czechoslovakian border patrol soldiers boarded the train. After collecting our visas, they left without any explanations. That made us feel very uncomfortable; we were left without any documents and were almost panicky when the train began to move. There were no soldiers, no conductors, and the doors on both sides were locked. The panic was growing to a degree that someone in our group even suggested pulling the emergency brake. An hour later, two soldiers unlocked one of the doors, called out our names, and handed our visas back to us. It was a great relief for all of us. As they were leaving, they told us that soon we would reach the Austrian border. We were getting very excited. Shortly the train stopped, and we saw the soldiers getting off the train.

Again, as it had happened in Russia, our conductor became a different person when the soldiers left; he immediately unlocked the doors and became pretty friendly, talking to us in almost perfect Russian. He gave us some advice about Austrian border patrol agents and about places to visit in Vienna. His explanation to us was the same as the explanation the Russian conductor had given us—he couldn't afford to lose this job and weekly trips to Vienna.

In less than fifteen minutes the train stopped again, this time for the Austrian border patrol soldiers to board the train. It was a very special moment in our lives. We felt very happy about entering the free world. There was nothing that could spoil this moment, not even the uncertainty of our future. My family and I had made it to the free world, and that was huge.

Chapter 8

The Austrian soldiers who boarded our train were dressed in special uniforms with bulletproof vests and Israeli Uzi machine guns. They looked very tough but were all smiles when boarding our train. None of us spoke German, however because the German language was close to the Yiddish language, our knowledge of Yiddish helped. We could understand quite a few words and even tried to communicate with them. I really don't remember what we were trying to tell them; all I remember very well is how the soldiers were trying so hard to understand us and their happy reactions when we understood some of their words. Every time we could make out some of what they said, they cheered and showed okay hand signals to us. It was a very different experience—the soldiers didn't scream or intimidate us, and we felt that they were there to help us.

After checking our visas, the soldiers went to the exit doors and stood there with their guns down. We were in Austria, and I remember how all of us were trying to look through the windows—we wanted to see what freedom looked like. It was very late, I was extremely tired but couldn't sleep. My mind was working hard thinking of the immediate steps we needed to take upon arrival to Vienna.

According to the information we got from people who went through this before us, we knew that upon arrival to Vienna the Israeli agents from Sohnut would try very hard to convince us to go to Israel. The plan was for Sophia and Robby to stay with the luggage while I located Hebrew Immigrant Aid Society (HIAS) representatives who were also supposed to be at the railroad station and let them know about our plans to go to America.

Based on the advice of the people who had left before us, I knew that Sohnut people would try to discourage us from going to America and would do their best to take possession of our visas. Because of that I had to act quickly and hand our visas to the HIAS people so they would act as our guides and protectors. We knew that HIAS would also help us with housing, food, and most importantly, until the Italian government allowed us to travel to Italy, they would help with the necessary paperwork during our stay in Vienna. We knew that HIAS had permission from both the Austrian and Italian governments to help us.

The people we met in Bratislava were also planning to go to America, so we planned to stick together until one of us got in touch with the HIAS representative.

Suddenly the train stopped, but it wasn't at the railroad station. A Russian-speaking man boarded the train, and after welcoming us to the free world, he asked us to unload all of our suitcases. That wasn't consistent with any information we knew. When we asked for an explanation, the man had only one answer to all of our questions. His answer was that just last week the Austrian government had implemented a new procedure, and we shouldn't worry about anything. We had no choice but to unload our suitcases. A few men outside picked up our suitcases and loaded them onto a truck. Our worries increased even more when we were told that all of our suitcases would be waiting for us at the hotel. The best explanation given to us was that this would expedite our move through the railroad station, and that all of this was done strictly for security reasons.

Our worries worsened after we found out that the Russian man was a representative of Sohnut. We were pretty certain that this was the new tactic Sohnut was using to make us go to Israel, however we had no choice but to follow his directions. As soon as our luggage was placed on the truck, we were moving again and soon arrived at Vienna's main railroad station. During that time, we were planning how we would make sure that at least one of us would find the HIAS representatives and tell them that Sohnut had all of our luggage. We knew that HIAS people should have visible HIAS badges.

As we were looking through the window, we didn't see any HIAS representatives outside, and all of us were panicking. Two more Austrian soldiers with machine guns approached our railroad car, and we were asked by the Russian to leave the train, stay together, and follow him. Our visas were with the Austrian soldiers, and when we asked for them, the Russian-speaking man told us again not to worry, that we'd get them at the hotel.

At that time, I didn't have a choice but to disclose to the Sohnut person about our intentions to go to America and not Israel. I also told him that we didn't want to go to Sohnut's hotel. His answer to me was that he understood our request, however due to the Austrian government's request, the procedure had been changed a few days earlier, and all Jews passing through Austria had to stay in one central place. When I asked what would happen if we refused to go with him, his answer was that we had no documents, no rights in this country, and should we refuse to follow the directions, the police could arrest us and possibly deport us back to the country we arrived from. At the same time, he was trying to assure us that we'd still be able to go to America if that was our choice.

After this short standoff, we realized that we had no choice but to follow his instructions. On the way to our bus we were kept together, and there were at least five soldiers with machine guns escorting us. Two of the soldiers boarded the bus with us. We were so upset that we didn't even look through the bus windows to enjoy Vienna's beautiful night views.

Years later I couldn't recall anything from that bus trip except being very upset, soldiers with guns on our bus, and two police cars escorting our bus. We felt that we were trapped and were forced to go to Israel against our will. Our bus trip lasted about thirty minutes, and when the bus stopped, we were somewhere outside of Vienna in front of a big castle. There were soldiers guarding the entrance as our bus entered the castle. At that point, we understood that we had no chance to see anyone except Sohnut personnel and had no other choice than to comply with their orders.

As we were leaving the bus, our Russian translator was again assuring us that within a few days we would be able to proceed to our chosen destinations. As we went inside, Sophia and I held hands with Robby, and we had no idea what to expect. When we entered, Russian Jewish people who welcomed us to the free world surrounded us. The room walls were covered with Israeli flags, pictures of Jerusalem, and other Israeli sites. Israeli music was playing. Even though we were very tense because of all the uncertainty surrounding us, it didn't take long before Sophia and I were completely immersed in the very happy and relaxing atmosphere. We felt at home, we hugged each other and everyone who welcomed us. For the first time in our lives we were welcomed as Jews and had the feeling that we were safe, and nobody could hurt us. Somehow we also got the feeling that eventually we would end up in America.

We were directed to go to a dining hall where the food was already on the tables, waiting for us. Nobody in our group knew that this was the first day of Hanukkah. Israelis were celebrating, and they made a special effort to show and explain to us what this holiday meant for Jewish people. All I knew about Hanukkah was the "Hanukkah gelt" that my grandparents and parents had given us during the wintertime. As we entered the hall, our kids received dreidels, gold chocolate coins, and there was a lot of traditional Jewish food and kosher red wine on the table. It felt very good; it felt like we were home.

After the meal, we were led to a large room with beds. About thirty people were asleep there, our beds were ready, and I was looking forward to a good long night of sleep. We were very tired, and the fact that there were other people sleeping in the same room didn't bother us a bit. While on the train to Vienna, Robby didn't feel well, and we had thought he was simply tired. As we were getting ready to go to bed his condition worsened, and he was running a high fever. I called for help, and almost immediately a doctor showed up. We went to the medical office, and after checking Robby the doctor didn't seem to be concerned. He told us it was probably a virus and in a few days Robby would be better. In order to bring his fever down, instead of a traditional pill he used a suppository. We'd never seen this and were shocked when the doctor did it. To our surprise it worked very quickly, and as we held Robby in our arms walking back to the sleeping room, his fever dropped in a very short time to a manageable level. Both Sophia and I watched Robby, making sure he was okay, and neither of us had a chance to get any sleep.

As everyone around us woke up, we were very anxious to ask them about the new Austrian rules, and if we would still have a chance to go to the USA. The very first person I asked assured me that five days prior to our arrival, based on the terrorist threats and illegal sales by the people from Russia, the Austrian government had made this change. They didn't want us to be on the streets of Vienna, so they made us stay in this castle until we moved either to Israel or to Italy. He also told us that instead of spending the usual month in Vienna, we would be transported to Italy within five days.

Next we were very anxious to find out where Sam and his family were. When we asked about them, we were told that according to the information Sohnut received, Sam and his family would be arriving here that night. All that information, together with Robby's quick recovery, made us feel relaxed, and we truly enjoyed our first day of being in the free world.

Indeed, after dinner, we were told that the bus carrying Sam's family was going to arrive shortly. Sophia and I went outside to meet them, and it was a pretty emotional and happy reunion. All of us were very happy to see each other. Earlier in the day I was assured that our families would be leaving the castle together regardless of the fact that Sam and his family arrived later than we did. The Sohnut personnel were trained to do their best to try to convince people to go to Israel, especially when working with younger, well-educated people. We, however, were very determined about our intent to go to America. Our argument to them was that from America, we would be able to go to Israel at any time. Conversely, going to Israel would have made our move to America almost impossible.

The biggest reason that the move to America from Israel was impossible was the tab the Israeli government immediately opened from the moment people agreed to go to Israel. From that moment everything, including the stay in the castle, was added to the tab. Under normal circumstances, the bill would run up to around $10,000, and it was forgiven unless the people chose to leave Israel. In order to leave people had to repay the Israeli government this amount.

I remember the guilty feeling we all had when refusing their numerous attempts to change our minds. We knew were in the free world because of Israel; we also knew that only in Israel were Jews first-class citizens, and most of us also remembered our grandparents' prayers about "next year in Jerusalem."

However, all that guilt couldn't overcome our original decision to go to America, where in addition to not being persecuted for being Jewish, we would have a better opportunity to establish ourselves. As we were waiting for our departure, the Israelis used every moment to convince us that Israel needed us and that we needed Israel even more. Most of the workers were from the Soviet Union; they were working with us on an individual basis. In addition, on different occasions movie clips about Israel and the way the Israeli government takes care of Russian immigrants was shown to the entire group. We were told a lot about the worry-free process from that moment until we found jobs in Israel versus the difficulties we would face from day one in America.

Though we knew that this was true, we also knew that we would not be left alone should we stick to our decision to go to America. We knew that HIAS would take care of us in Italy, and they would help us to get refugee status and find a Jewish community in America to sponsor us. We also knew that the Jewish community in America would help us during the first three months; they would find a place for us to live, and Jewish volunteers would be assigned to guide us through the first few steps in getting settled there. So for us, the biggest difference between going to Israel or America was the challenge of finding a job in America by ourselves.

Among those of us who were trying to make it to America were families whose relatives there would sponsor the newcomers. There were families who had friends in America, who would have to come up with money for the Federation to sponsor newcomers. For us the choices were Sophia's mother's cousins in Philadelphia or our friends in Los Angeles. Sophia's mother's cousins, whose father was Sophia's grandfather's brother, had left Russia in 1920. His daughters were born in America. Over the years when their father was still alive, they had communicated with Sophia's family, and their father even visited Beltsy once. Sophia's mom insisted on us contacting them to ask if they would sponsor us. While in Rome we called, but after hearing them say that they could sponsor only one family, we decided that Philadelphia wasn't an option for us.

Our friends Mark and Sofia, who had been struggling for two years to become medical doctors in Los Angeles, after checking were told by the Federation that a $2,500 per person donation including children was required in order for us to be sponsored by them. Our friends didn't have that kind of money, they would have to borrow it and we would have to pay it back. It was a quick decision—we didn't want to start our life in America with a large debt, so we declined the option to go to Los Angeles. We knew that there would be a community in America that would accept us as is.

Chapter 9

I remember our last night in Vienna—it was around three a.m. when I woke up thinking how much easier it would be for us to go to Israel. I walked up to the window overlooking a street outside the castle and saw soldiers with machine guns walking around the castle, protecting us. It felt very secure; we were inside a protected, safe place, I didn't have to think about how to provide for my family, and I could have all that by simply agreeing to go to Israel. In contrast to that, should we continue with our plan to go to America, within a few hours we would lose all that security. As soon as we were out of Sohnut's protection, I would be the one to find a way to provide for my family in a very unfamiliar environment. We would end up in a place without any family or friends, not knowing the country's culture or their language. We would have to find jobs by ourselves, and I would be the safety net for my wife and son. It was scary because we had nobody behind us; there was no safety net for me. I was only twenty-six years old, and all of that was quite a responsibility for a young man like me, who had almost no practical life experience.

This was the first time I had thoughts like that, and I think it happened mainly because for the last few days the Jewish people and Jewish culture, as well as the excellent work done by Sohnut personnel, surrounded us. They were putting doubts in our minds and actually making some of the families change their plans and go to Israel. I, however, decided to stick to our original plan and proceed with our journey to America.

As soon as Sohnut people realized that they couldn't change our decision, their attitude toward us changed completely. Our bus to the Vienna railroad station was scheduled to leave in the evening, and for the whole day nobody even spoke to us. After dinner we were asked not to leave the room. Shortly after, a Russian-speaking man came in to talk to us. It was Sohnuts' last chance to change our minds and reroute some of us to Israel. The man, who was in his fifties, told us terrifying stories about our soon-to-begin journey to America. First, he told us we would end up on a train from Vienna to Rome, similar to the trains the Nazis used during WWII when they transported Jews with the doors and the windows shut, and that we wouldn't be allowed to get off the train, even if we needed to. Second, he told us that because Italians didn't like Russian Jews, they would, upon our arrival to Rome, keep our suitcases for as long they could to prevent us from selling and making extra money from the tools, optics, and other items we had brought with us. He finished his speech with a statement that although Jews in America don't feel that they are second-class citizens, a lot of Americans still don't like Jews, and the only place for us to be was Israel. At the beginning of his speech, when he was talking about the train, I felt terrified. As his speech progressed, I understood that a lot of what he said was just a last-minute effort to change our decision, and the information he was telling us was not very accurate.

Actually, for me, this speech worked against Sohnut, and when he finished talking, I felt very angry with them. Instead of changing our minds, this last-minute attempt made our decision of not going to Israel even stronger.

Altogether, there were seven families leaving the castle that evening. The bus arrived around six p.m., and after our suitcases were loaded we were told to proceed to the bus. To our surprise, Sohnut people gave us packages with food, wishing us a safe trip and good luck in America.

Again, as on the way to the castle, there were two police cars escorting us with two soldiers sitting on our bus. All the way to the railroad station, Sophia and I looked through the window at the beautiful Vienna scenery. We made a promise to each other to come back to Vienna when we could afford it.

At the railroad station, there were a few more soldiers waiting for us. We were told to move toward the train as quickly as we could. The soldiers stayed next to us, and we were almost running. All that was done for our protection, as there had been incidents in the past when Russian Jews on the way to Israel had been attacked and even killed.

As soon as we were inside the train, the soldiers closed the door; they stayed outside while a Russian-speaking man boarded the train. He had our visas, called us one by one, and handed them to us, telling us that as soon as our luggage was placed inside, the soldiers would lock the doors for our protection. Shortly after our luggage was inside, the soldiers locked the doors and placed some metal bars across them, exactly as the Sohnut person told us it would happen. It felt very uncomfortable, and even though I knew that it was for our own protection, I felt trapped. There were three or four more cars on the train but we couldn't go there, and nobody could come to our car. Before leaving the train, the Sohnut man told us that our car was stocked with food and drinks, and there was a conductor available, should we need his help.

Shortly after midnight our train finally left Vienna. All of the adults were awake, talking, expressing concerns, and guessing about our next steps in Italy and America. When we finally went to our compartment, Sophia and I looked at our sleeping son and instantly got the feeling that no matter how hard it would be in the beginning, he would have a much better life simply because he wouldn't be persecuted just for being Jewish. He would be able to be whoever he wanted to be and not what the government wanted him to be.

I fell asleep and woke up when the train stopped. It was a very dark night; there were only a few lights outside, in front of our train. I had no idea why we were not moving until an Italian soldier came in. He knew a few Russian words and welcomed us to Italy. He asked for our visas. When we handed our visas to him, we were told that we would get them back in Rome. He also told us that for our own protection, he would stay with us until we arrived in Rome. He tried to have a conversation with us, but his Russian vocabulary was very limited.

As he was talking I suddenly realized that I understood a lot of words, which was because Italian is quite similar to the Romanian/Moldavian language. Between Sam and me, we could get a general understanding of what he was trying to tell us. However, when we tried to answer in Romanian, he couldn't understand us.

This was the first time since we left Russia that we couldn't communicate with people. In Bratislava, most people knew Russian, and in Vienna Russians surrounded us. Now we were facing a new reality—the inability to communicate; however, it didn't scare us very much. We knew that the language barrier would be much easier to overcome compared to the other issues we were facing. The Italian soldier saw our concerns and was trying very hard to communicate to us that everything would be okay. He was smiling, shaking our hands, and giving us hugs. His efforts, along with the beautiful scenery of the snowy Alps, finally calmed us down.

As it happened in Vienna, our luggage was unloaded before we reached the railroad station. When we reached the station, there were a few armed soldiers on the platform waiting for us. We were allowed to leave the train only after everyone else left. Outside, on the platform, there were a few Russian-speaking men together with more soldiers, and it was a relief for us to hear the language we understood. They told us that they were the HIAS representatives and that we shouldn't worry about anything. They told us that they had arranged for a place for us to stay and that HIAS would be helping us with the preparation of all of the necessary paperwork we would need for the American Embassy. They also told us that unlike Vienna, nothing had been changed in Rome. In addition, they said that due to increased terrorist threats, the Italian government had amplified security in areas where we were an easy target, including the railroad station, the HIAS office, and the American Consulate and that was the reason we saw a lot of soldiers.

After a short bus ride, we arrived at a hotel that became our home for the next two weeks. It was a small hotel, our room was clean, and we were fed three times a day. For the first time in a week, we enjoyed being in a separate room that we didn't have to share with others. Within an hour of our arrival, we were told that our luggage had arrived, and it was located in the backyard of the hotel.

I remember how all of the men formed a human chain, passing the suitcases to each other, and very quickly all of our suitcases were in the rooms. As we were moving our suitcases, a few Russian-speaking men came to the hotel, asking us about the photo equipment we had brought with us. Offering American dollars, they tried to convince us to sell the equipment. I actually knew the approximate amounts some photo equipment could be sold for, and when one of man offered to buy it for an amount close to the one I knew, I made the decision to sell one camera. Later I realized that I could have sold that camera for an extra $50.00, however I have never regretted my decision to sell on spot. By getting some money right away we gained the ability to buy food, soda, and everything else we couldn't buy in Russia, and that was more important for me at that time. I also remember the feeling of being rich; I sold the camera for $260 and was paid with two $100.00 bills and three $20.00 bills.

It took us almost the whole day to get situated in the hotel, and after dinner we went for a walk. It was beautiful to walk at night on the streets of Rome. The next morning, we woke up to the aroma of freshly baked bread. Breakfast was served at seven-thirty a.m. and we were offered fresh bread, butter, jelly, and cereal with milk.

Closer to lunchtime, HIAS people arrived to give us an overview of the procedures and schedules between now and the time we would board the plane to America. They also told us that for the next few days there were no scheduled activities for us. We were left alone to enjoy our true freedom, and we used this time to familiarize ourselves with Rome. This marked another very important moment in our lives; we were walking the streets of Rome without any supervision. We had neither plans nor maps; we were just walking the streets of Rome, recognizing some historical places.

Later in the week it was time for us to sign more paperwork, and we were asked to come to the HIAS office. When we were ready to leave, HIAS representatives give us Italian money to pay for the bus ride back to our hotel. Most of us decided to save the money and walked instead, and it took us about an hour to make it there. It was a beautiful late morning; we stopped at a coffee shop to buy real Italian espresso with the saved transportation money, and what a treat that was for us!

At the beginning of our second week we had to go again to the HIAS office to complete and sign a lot more paperwork. Upon completing the paperwork, we were handed our weekly allowance check. It was calculated on a $5 per day per person allowance, and it included transportation as well as miscellaneous expenses. During this visit, we were also told that our stay in the hotel would be over by the beginning of the next week, and it was our responsibility to find a place to rent and move there. The easiest and best area for us to rent a place would be in Rome, however the rent in Rome was very expensive. At the HIAS office we were told about two cities where the majority of people like us were staying. We were also told that Ladispoli was a nicer place. The trains from the Rome Terminal station were leaving every two hours, so we decided to go to Ladispoli to look around and rent a place.

In order to make some money, we had to sell all our photo equipment and the tools we brought with us. We knew that the best place to sell it was the flea market called Americana located in Rome. It was open on Saturdays and Sundays only. As the first Saturday approached, we decided to go there. Americana was quite a distance from our hotel, and in order to get a good space, we had to be there no later than six a.m. We didn't want to pay for a taxi, so Sam and I took two suitcases and left the hotel by four a.m. When we reached Americana by six o'clock, we found many Russian Jews trying to do the same thing—sell photo equipment and tools.

Because there were so many sellers, our first reaction was that it would be impossible to sell our equipment. To our surprise, all of the equipment we had in the suitcases was sold within two hours. I made over $800 and was very happy. We were back in the hotel by noon, and with the extra money we were able to afford to buy better food to enhance our hotel's menu, which offered similar things every day.

The next day, Sunday, all of us went to the train station, and after repeating the word Ladispoli a few times, the clerk finally issued tickets for us to board the train. Ladispoli is a small resort town on the Mediterranean Sea, and it took us about an hour and a half to get there. A lot of Russian families had chosen to stay in this town while waiting for permission to enter either the USA or other countries. We had no problem finding places for rent. In order to save money, we rented a one-bedroom apartment together with Sam. Our apartment was on the fourth floor of a nine-floor building, and it was located a few blocks from the beach. The apartment had a large balcony with a view of the Mediterranean Sea with the black sand beach.

The next weekend, we went back to Americana and sold more of the tools and equipment. While in Ladispoli, we returned to Americana a few more times to sell whatever was left. We actually had fun doing that; we would take the four a.m. train to Rome, walking from the train station to Americana and on the way back buying a cheap bottle of Chianti to drink on the train ride to Ladispoli.

In Ladispoli there was a club designed for Russian immigrants. Every day we would go there, share the latest news, and have a cup of coffee. The best part of the club was the library—it had all the books we'd heard about but weren't allowed to read in Russia. The first book I read was Solzhenitsyn's *The Gulag Archipelago*, and it was quite an experience. I also remember how fascinated I was reading books about the communist leaders and the KGB. Today, this information means almost nothing, but at that time, getting to know all of the facts was very intriguing for us.

A few days after moving to Ladispoli, my twenty-seventh birthday was coming up. The day before my birthday, Sam and I went to Rome to buy food from the farmers' market, which was called the "round market". It was a great place to shop for food; mainly we'd been buying chicken wings—the cheapest meat. For my birthday, we decided to buy some beef. Since we'd never shopped in Italy for beef, we suddenly realized it wasn't that simple. There were so many varieties of meat that we couldn't determine which one was beef, pork, or lamb. We didn't know how to ask, nor could we understand what the vendors were telling us. After a few unsuccessful conversations we decided it was time to improvise. Sam picked up some meat from the table, looked at the vendor, and began to make the "moo" sound. It worked; the vendor laughed, answering "baa" in the same tone Sam had used. We understood that it was lamb. All of us had a good laugh, and after we bought the beef, the vendor wrapped the piece of lamb we originally picked up, placed it in our hands, and didn't charge us for it. Back in Ladispoli, Sophia and Janet prepared the meat, and we opened a bottle of red sparkling wine we brought with us from Russia. It was the first celebration we had in the free world, and it felt good.

Sophia, Robby, me

Robby, Sophia, Janet, Len, Mila

Robby, Sophia, me

Chapter 10

Since it was Christmastime, we were told by the HIAS people not to expect any action from the US Consulate until the beginning of the new year. We decided to use all that time to explore Italy. For the first time, we saw the beautiful and creative Christmas decorations on the streets and individual front yards. We also learned that Christmas trees are not the trees for the New Year celebrations, and also, that the New Year's celebration is not a big holiday in Italy. Conversely, New Year's celebrations were among the biggest non-political holidays in Russia, with similar decorations being used for the New Year's celebration in Russia, as people used for Christmas here in Italy. Without knowing a lot about Christmas, everyone in Russia, including Jews, would decorate trees for New Year's celebration.

A few days into the new year, our HIAS representative informed us that both Sam's family and mine had to report to the US Embassy on January seventh. That was a very important, if not the most important, meeting with the Americans. During this meeting they usually would make the decision to allow or deny the opportunity for us to come to America. We knew of some cases when people weren't allowed entrance to America, but unfortunately no one knew the reasons for such rejections. There were speculations that if people or their immediate family members were associated with the Communist Party or had any criminal records, they would not be allowed into America. Americans were checking our knowledge of the Jewish religion. Even though we had nothing to hide and our Russian background was clear—neither we nor our parents or grandparents had been members of the

Communist Party, nor did any of us have any criminal records—we were still very nervous.

The day before our visit to the embassy we were asked to come to the HIAS, where we were informed and instructed about the usual procedures at the US Embassy. We also knew that if we were denied entrance to the USA, we would still have a choice to go to Israel, Canada, Australia, or New Zealand.

The next morning, we arrived at the embassy much earlier than requested, and for the first time, I saw a marine. He was in front of the gate, and even though he didn't smile and had a cold look, somehow it felt good and secure to have him next to us. After another marine checked our IDs, we were let into the building where a sign welcomed visitors to the USA. A few minutes later, Sam and I were asked to follow a man who spoke very good Russian. He introduced and identified himself as a CIA officer, then briefly explained what the CIA does and the reasons they wanted to talk to us. He asked Sam to move to another room, and then asked me to tell him about my army experience. As he was getting the army information, he was also trying to determine if I was really of Jewish descent, and if I was really telling the truth. Later we were told that during the last few years there had been cases of Russians trying to send in spies by pretending to be Russian Jews asking for political refugee status. The majority of our conversation was focused on my Jewish background. He asked the same questions in different forms and wrote down all of my answers. He wasn't interested in my military information due to my uneventful army experience and quickly joined another officer who was interviewing Sam.

Since Sam had actually spent two years in the army, his interview was much longer, and he was even asked to come back for an additional interview. After they were done with the army information, Sophia, Janet, and our kids were brought into the room. Another Russian-speaking person entered the room and began asking questions about our reasons for choosing the USA as our final destination. He was asking how we were persecuted in Russia, why we didn't want to go to Israel, and why none of our parents were coming with us. After hearing our answers, he thanked us and left the room. A few minutes later a different person entered the room and asked us almost identical questions. We were confused and couldn't understand why different people were asking us the same questions time after time. Only years later, when I was working in the nuclear industry and had to take psychological tests, did I realize that asking the same questions over and over and comparing the answers allows the interviewer to determine if you are being truthful.

Finally, we were told that the interview was over, and we were free to go. On the way out we were told to expect the US government decision within a few weeks.

Back in Ladispoli, there was nothing much for us to do, and that's when a Russian-speaking guide offered us a two-day bus tour either to the northern or southern areas of Italy. We couldn't afford both, so we decided that Sophia and I would go to the northern part of the country, visiting Pisa, Venice, and Florence, and Sam and Janet would go to the south. It was a very memorable trip for us, even though we didn't have enough money to buy souvenirs or try the food we wanted to try.

During our stop in Pisa, we walked up the stairs of the Leaning Tower even though the TV cameras were continuously rolling to record when it fell down. It wasn't even a year after we had been there that the tours were suspended for safety reasons. We can say that we were among the last people to be on the top of the tower. In Pisa, we also experienced for the first time the taste of a pizza. In Russia, we'd never heard of pizza, and the only reason we had ordered pizza was the price—it was the cheapest item on the menu at a restaurant across the square from the Leaning Tower. We also couldn't resist ordering a cup of fresh strawberries with whipped cream because fresh strawberries in January were very unreal for us.

Next stop was Florence. We went to a few museums where we could get in at no charge; we also walked the streets and plazas of Florence for hours. Finally, we ended up at the Academy of Arts, where the sculpture of David was displayed. The tickets were not cheap, but we didn't care, we had to see it. It was a great experience; we spent a few hours there looking at the sculpture from every direction.

Venice was also a remarkable place to visit; it was an amazing experience to see so much history and beauty in one place. When we saw the gondola with the singing gondolier, Sophia and I wanted to take a ride. We didn't, because the tickets were $25 each, and it was way too much for us to spend. There was, however, one purchase we made in Venice. When passing by a jewelry store, Sophia and I spotted a Star of David necklace, and instantly I knew that I had to have it. We also purchased a gold chain from which to hang the star. I placed it on my neck and didn't remove it for many years. However, that purchase took all of the money we had on us. We had to borrow some money to buy some toys for Robby and Sam's kids, Len and Mila.

A few weeks after our interview with the Americans, we were contacted by HIAS with the news that the US government made a decision to allow both of our families to enter America as political refugees. It is impossible to describe the feelings of relief we all had upon receiving such news. It felt great.

As we were waiting for the American government's decision, HIAS was actively trying to find a Jewish community in the USA that would sponsor both of our families for the first three months of our arrival.

We told our HIAS guide that we'd go wherever the US government wanted to send us, without having to pay for it. Three days later we were told to be at the HIAS office, where our guide told us that the Jewish community of Houston had agreed to sponsor both of our families.

At that time, all we knew about the city of Houston was its relationship with NASA. We didn't even know exactly where Houston was located, and of course we had no idea that Houston was the petrochemical center of America. I remember going to the library on the second floor of the HIAS office and trying to locate Houston on the map of the USA. When we found Houston, our first reaction was that it should be a good place—it was close to the Gulf of Mexico and far from New York City. As we were waiting to sign the papers, a young man who was a helper to our HIAS guide told us again that the Jewish community in Houston had accepted us. After telling him that we were very happy because of the city size and its geographical location, he looked a little puzzled. He told us that we'd located the wrong city on the map, and the city we were going to was a little town in Illinois. He explained that Houston in Texas has the letter U and is pronounced with the "OU" sound. The town in Illinois was so small that it was shown only on the map of Illinois, and not the US.

Suddenly we became very concerned. We were afraid that going to a small town would make it very hard for us to find jobs. We went to our guide, who had an office on the third floor, for an explanation. She began laughing and assured us that we were going to Houston, Texas, and also explained to us that in addition to being accepted by the Jewish Federation, it should be a great place for us to find jobs. That's when we learned about the petrochemical industry and the great need for engineering-skilled professionals there. We were also told that our departure date had already been set for January twenty-first. All of that news was very exciting for us. We finally knew the place where and the date when we'd be going to America.

Chapter 11

Our flight was scheduled to depart Rome in the afternoon, and we were told that the bus would pick us up from the central plaza in Ladispoli at six a.m. We were so excited that none of us could sleep, and by five a.m., we were on the way to the meeting place. At the airport we met a few more Russian families who were flying to America on the same flight. Some of them were relaxed because they were going to their relatives or friends. Some, like us, were very tense, because we were going to be on our own from the beginning. In general, all of us were very happy. We were on our way to a new life, new beginnings, and a lot of new challenges.

As we were waiting, we learned that the Italian airport workers and the Italian airline went on strike, but since we were flying Pan American, our flight would depart from Rome as scheduled. After a short delay we boarded the plane, flight #111 to New York. I'd never been on any planes except the Russian mid-size planes. The plane we boarded was a Boeing 747. It was huge and very impressive, and the flight attendants were very friendly. They smiled and talked to us; unfortunately we couldn't understand them. Sitting across the aisle from us was a Polish couple returning home to America from their visit to Poland. We could understand some of the Polish words, and they could understand Russian words, so we asked them to help us communicate with the flight attendants. In our conversations with them, they told us that life in New York is much more similar to life in Europe, but that the people in Texas are much nicer than people in New York. It was very comforting for us to hear good things about Texas people.

After dinner, a movie was shown on the large screen; we watched without understanding it and got ready to take a nap. We were about six hours into the flight. Suddenly all of the lights went off, the emergency lights and sirens went on, and the oxygen masks fell down. The plane began a very rapid descent, and it felt almost like a free fall. We had to grab Robby and Sam's kids and buckle them up. The situation was very scary. People were screaming, and most of us were pretty sure that we were going to crash into the Atlantic Ocean. About two or three minutes into the rapid descent, to our relief, we felt that the plane was also moving forward faster than it was going down. However, it didn't help to calm the situation when the smell of burned fuel got into the cabin. We were pretty sure that there was a fire somewhere. It also didn't help that no flight attendants were visible, and no announcements were made.

After all these years, I clearly remember the hopeless feeling I had. I felt terrible because I knew that I wouldn't be able to help my wife and son when we hit the water. In my mind, we were going to die, and even if the plane didn't break up on impact, we would freeze in the cold water of the Atlantic in the middle of January. On the contrary, Sophia was sure we were going to be okay and was trying to find life jackets and learn how to use them. I panicked—I grabbed and hugged Sophia and Robby. Reflections of many moments of my life went through my mind during that time, and I also thought how sad it was that we'd never be able to see America. Deep inside of me, I was hoping that some miracle would happen and we'd be saved, but as time passed, I lost hope and started accepting the fact that this was the end. As I was ready to face the worst, suddenly the cabin lights came on, and the captain made an announcement. Our neighbors, the Polish people, explained to us that one of the doors had gotten loose, causing the cabin to depressurize. To avoid a catastrophe, the pilot had to drop very quickly to a lower altitude and also requested an emergency landing on a Newfoundland military base.

We were lucky that it had all happened in close proximity to Newfoundland and that there was enough fuel to reach the airport flying at a much lower than normal altitude. We were flying very low; we could very clearly see the water. After flying low for almost an hour, the pilot informed us that we would land in about ten minutes. I still couldn't believe that we are going to be okay; we were getting closer and closer to the water without seeing any signs of land. It didn't help when Sophia pointed to the door flying away from the plane. The temperature in the cabin was dropping, I was preparing for the worst, and even Sophia began to lose her calm. We were very close to the water without seeing any land. Suddenly, when we were only about 300 feet above the water, we saw land below us, and within seconds the plane landed. What a feeling it was! We realized that we had survived and would be okay. A lot of people on the plane were crying, and most of us couldn't believe we were alive and safe on the ground. I felt like we had been born again, and it was a beautiful feeling. I remember that everything around us looked great, we were holding Robby, Sam and his family were together with us, and we were enjoying every second of life.

As the plane came to a stop, we saw a lot of emergency equipment and military personnel. There was at least five feet of snow on the ground and it was very cold, but nothing could spoil our celebration of being alive and safe. There was a lot of food and drinks waiting for us at the terminal. The drinks were going fast, and soon there were quite a few happy people sharing their experience with each other. A few hours later the captain made an announcement, telling us that Pan Am was searching for a replacement plane to send, while personnel at the base were making a temporary fix to our plane, just in case there were no replacement planes available. The pilot also explained that the plane had no mechanical problems and that in his mind the accident happened because the ground personnel in Rome had made some mistakes.

After having a few drinks, Sam and I went to the restroom. To our surprise, every single toilet in the restroom was broken—there was standing water in each of them. We were also very surprised that even though all of them were broken, there was no bad urine smell at the restroom. As we were standing there a man came in, used and flushed the toilet. We were expecting to see the water overflow, but nothing happened. When we made it back, Sophia and Janet told us the same story. It was our first experience with the standards of living in America, and we began to realize that we'd have to learn a lot right off the bat.

A few hours later the pilot told us that the airline couldn't find a replacement plane and that the next one wouldn't be available for another thirty-six hours. Based on that and the temporary fixes made by the base personnel, the captain made a decision to fly the same plane to New York. He determined that it was safe enough to fly at a low altitude and a very low speed after a temporary door was installed. Normally it is a one-and-a-half-hour flight between Newfoundland and New York, but it took us almost three and a half hours to get there.

When we arrived nine hours late to New York, there were a lot of people waiting. They knew about our accident, and everyone was happy we had arrived safely. At the airport, there were also people waiting for us; they were Sam's friends who had left Kishinev six months prior to our departure and were residing in Virginia.

Sophia and I had tears in our eyes when the American Customs agents said, "Welcome to America" after checking our papers. This moment brought so much happiness to us, nothing—starting with the three years of hell in Russia and ending with the plane accident a few hours ago—mattered anymore. We had finally made it to America!!!

Because of the delay, our flight to Houston was rescheduled for the following day. Russian-speaking HIAS personnel told us that we'd spend the night in New York and be on the way to Houston the next day. After a short bus ride, we arrived at the hotel. We were overwhelmed by the amount of lights, large cars, and limos surrounding us. HIAS people walked with us to our rooms and asked us to be ready to leave the hotel by ten a.m. After giving us $25 to buy food, they left. We were alone in America, and we felt very uncertain.

After Robby fell asleep, Sophia and I decided to get some food. We went downstairs and found a restaurant with live music. The music was loud, and there was a lot of smoke, but it was America, and everything looked perfect to us. As soon as we sat down, the waiter offered us the menu, and we pretended that we knew what we were looking for. In reality, we were only looking at the prices, trying to compare the dollar amounts to rubles. We knew that $25 was a weekly salary for us in Russia, so we felt rich and couldn't imagine spending even $5 for a dinner. This was also our first true restaurant experience outside of Russia. To our surprise, the cheapest item on the menu was $8.50, and it was for a salad. We decided to order and split one salad, and since we had never tried a Coke, we ordered one, for a total price of a little over $10.

Salads in Russia were made with tomatoes, cucumbers, and onions; the salad we got turned out to have a few tomatoes, a few slices of onions, and a lot of green leaves with raw mushrooms on top. We didn't know about the green leaves, and we didn't touch the raw mushrooms, because in Russia nobody in their right mind would eat raw mushrooms. We were sure they had made a mistake but didn't know how to ask. In addition, there was no oil in the salad, and we didn't know about the dressings that were on our table. Sophia and I ate the tomatoes and onions, finished the Coke, and paid the amount on the bill. We were very hungry and confused when we left. The waiter wasn't happy either; we didn't know about tips and of course didn't leave any.

In the morning, the HIAS person picked us up from the hotel and drove us to JFK. We bought food for our children but didn't want to spend money on ourselves, so we were pretty hungry when we boarded the plane. When the plane took off, we realized that because of our experience the previous day, flying wasn't fun anymore. Soon drinks and food were served, and after having a few drinks and some food, we felt better and more relaxed.

As we approached Houston we looked through the window, trying to see how Houston looked from the air. The strange thing was that the plane was about to land, but we still couldn't find any high-rise buildings. We couldn't see any city buildings at all, as a matter of fact. All we saw was empty land and a few farmhouses. After we landed, we put on warm clothes and hats before stepping off the plane. People looked and smiled at us, some trying to tell us something, but we couldn't understand them. As we walked from the plane to the terminal, we felt very warm air around us and thought that it was probably done intentionally, so people wouldn't feel cold during the winter. As we walked to the terminal our kids got hot. They were crying, asking us to remove their warm clothes. We had no choice but to remove their hats and coats, and very soon we had to remove ours as well. It didn't make any sense to us why was it so warm in January.

We were expecting to see some Russian-speaking people meeting us, but instead we saw a black man with a Russian sign asking us to follow him. He didn't speak any Russian, but we followed him to the luggage area, picked up our suitcases, and followed him to the exit. We couldn't believe how warm it was outside—it was sunny and sixty-five degrees, nothing we were used to in January. We followed the man to a bus, loaded our luggage, and boarded the bus without knowing where it would take us.

As we drove away from the airport, we quickly realized how different everything was—both the road and the cars. We were amazed that there were no traffic lights, and the bus was driving without any stops. Finally, after twenty minutes of the ride, we saw high-rise buildings and were sure that this was the place we would end up. To our surprise, the bus didn't stop, it was moving away from the city. We were confused, but without any English, all we could do was hope that the driver knew what he was doing. After another twenty minutes' ride, we ended up driving on some streets with traffic lights. It felt like we were in a city, but there were no high-rise buildings.

Finally, the bus stopped, we were asked to step out and found ourselves at a bus stop on Braeswood Street. There were two women who spoke to us in English and also had a Russian language sign saying that they were from the Jewish Federation. The sign identified them as Mrs. R. and Mrs. W. They were very friendly, hugged us, and asked us to get in their cars. The bus driver helped to load our suitcases into their cars, and we were on our way to the apartments on Gasmer Street.

Chapter 12

Mark

We had never seen an apartment complex before and couldn't understand where we were. We were confused— to us, the apartment complex looked like military barracks. Only after the ladies opened the apartment doors and asked us to come in did we realize that this was the place where we would live. Our apartment was on the second floor, Sam's was on the first, and both apartments were two-bedroom units. We had never seen anything like this before; there was no entrance hall, so right away we walked into the living room, and the kitchen was just behind it. There was some furniture in the living room: a table with four chairs, a sofa, and an armchair. The women opened the refrigerator, showing us the food they had purchased for us. There was a whole chicken, fresh fruits and vegetables, milk, and a bottle of Coke. We also found all the necessary kitchenware and baking needs. After trying to tell us something in English, they finally gave up, and after handing us the apartment keys, they left. There was another Russian sign telling us that someone who spoke Russian would come to visit us later.

When we walked into the bedrooms, we found two sets of beds on the floor in each of the bedrooms. One was a comfortable mattress, and the second one very uncomfortable. We couldn't understand the purpose of two beds and were bothered about our beds being on the floor. There was another door in the bedroom, and when we opened it, we walked into a room without any windows. That became a mystery for us; we were trying to understand the purpose of a dark room. Sam's apartment had a different floor plan, but it also had the dark room and two beds in each bedroom.

We were also trying to understand why there were no light fixtures in the rooms, only floor lamps. As we tried to solve all of these mysteries, someone knocked on the door. When we opened the door, a Russian-speaking man who introduced himself as Efim, an immigrant from Russia who had arrived from Leningrad four months before us, came in.

Jewish Family Services had a policy ensuring that the latest arrivals would be greeted and introduced to the very basics by the people who arrived in Houston just prior to them. We were very happy to see Efim. He answered a lot of our questions but soon told us that he was tired after a long day at work and would be leaving soon. Before he left, we told him about our concerns regarding the mattresses being on the floor. He had a screwdriver with him and explained how to put the frames together, telling us to use the mattresses on top of the base. It felt great that we wouldn't have to sleep on the floor. The dark room mystery was also solved. We hadn't heard about walk-in closets in Russia, but now we had one. The information he gave us was very helpful and confusing at the same time. After telling us that opening a bank account as soon as possible should be our priority, he left.

We were lost; we didn't know anything about banking. In Russia, there were no checks. Everything from getting my salary to purchasing cars was done by cash only. He explained to us that we had to take the cash we had to a bank and open an account. The bank he mentioned was within walking distance of our apartments. After Efim left we felt even more confused.

As soon as we put the beds together we fell asleep. I woke up in the middle of the night and couldn't sleep anymore. I guess the reason for that was the combination of the time change and the uncertainty of our future. I felt very insecure and scared. This was our final destination, and unlike the other places on the way here, this was the place where we had to understand the culture, learn the language, and make it our home. The biggest concern for me was the fact that there was nobody I could rely on or ask in case my family needed anything. The only entity I knew that might help us was the Jewish Federation, so the JF of Houston became my security net.

In the morning, the same women who brought us here returned and drove us to the office of the Jewish Family Service on S. Braeswood. There were no Russian-speaking personnel at the office, and after signing the essential papers, we were told that for a few weeks there would be no more business for us—at least that's what we understood. On the way back, they drove past the bank to show us where it was. They also showed us two supermarkets, one of which, Weingarten, was next to the bank, and another, Blue Bonnet, was next to our apartment complex. After leaving their phone numbers and telling us to call if we needed to, they left.

The next day, we decided to check out the supermarket next to our apartments. We were expecting to walk into a store similar to those we had seen in Italy, but what we found when we entered was pretty shocking to us. It was a store much larger than any we'd ever seen, it had a lot of rows stocked with different products. We couldn't believe the variety of products, and for the next hour all we did was walk the aisles, checking out products. We couldn't believe the amount of meats on display—we were overwhelmed because buying meat in Russia was never that easy. The meat was never on display, and we always had to bribe the clerk in order to buy it.

We were shocked even more when we reached the produce department. In addition to the quality and quantity, we were impressed with the variety of fruits and vegetables. It was unbelievable to see such variety in the middle of the winter. In Russia, there were no fresh vegetables or fruits during wintertime. For us, this walk through the supermarket was equal to a museum experience. We didn't know that this was just a small grocery store in comparison to the large chains. A few months later, when we met the Chinese family who owned it, they told us that they were very suspicious when we were walking in their store for over an hour, picking up products from the shelves, looking at them, and putting them back without buying anything. We probably would have spent more time in the store, but Robby told me that he was thirsty.

On the way out of the store I saw a Coke machine and decided to buy Coke for Robby; however, I realized that I didn't know how to operate the machine. All of us were trying to figure how to get the can out of the machine. I felt helpless and frustrated, Robby began to cry, and I couldn't help him. As I picked Robby up, ready to go back to our apartments, a little black boy stopped at the machine, dropped in two coins, pushed a button and the can came out. I did the same as the little boy had done, and it worked; Robby got a Coke.

When we returned to our apartment, I closed myself in the bathroom and fought my streaming tears. This experience again proved that my concerns were valid. I didn't know anything here and would have to learn everything from scratch. I also knew that because I felt responsible for making Sophia and Robby feel secure, I couldn't show them my concerns, and it made it even harder to deal with. I remember this feeling very well; it was a feeling of being afraid of not having answers when my family asked.

We had a very small black and white TV, which was our only window to the news; however, no matter how hard we tried, we couldn't understand anything they were saying. It was very hard because I have always followed the world news, but since leaving Italy and having no interactions with any Russian sources of information, we had no idea what was going on; it felt like we were in a darkroom.

Because we were trying to get used to the American English language, we kept our TV on all day long. We brought with us an English study book and a few dictionaries, and on our second day we began to study English. Because we knew that this was the base for us to make it in America, we made it our number one priority. We also understood that without a car, we wouldn't survive in Houston, and that was quite a surprise for us. Our information on what to do and what to purchase at the start of our American life was based on the information from our Los Angeles friends. Because of the public transportation in Los Angeles, they didn't own a car. Conversely, there was almost no public transportation in Houston. Therefore, the driver's license book also became our priority.

On the third day in America, while Sophia and Robby were still asleep, I decided to go for a walk and explore our apartment complex. As I was walking toward the apartment's office, I passed by a man working on a large green car. He looked like a guy from Russia, and I asked him if he spoke Russian. To my great relief, he answered in Russian. His name was Mark, and he used to live in Minsk and had arrived in Houston about a month earlier. That connection grew stronger every day. Thirty-eight years later, we remain best friends and talk every day. During all those years—especially the first five years, when we went through a lot of tough times together—helping each other in difficult times made our friendship so strong that we consider ourselves family. Robby even calls him Uncle Mark.

Because Mark had already been in the country for over a month, he became an authority to me. Prior to Houston,

Mark spent time in Israel, which gave him another great advantage: living experience outside of Russia. Mark's friend, also from Minsk, had helped him move to Houston from New York, and Mark was sharing an apartment with another man who was also a Russian emigrant. Mark's roommate had been in the country for over one year and was a great source of information. I was very happy to find a Russian-speaking person, and Mark was also happy meeting us.

During our conversation Mark told me that he had never driven a car until the week before, and now after getting a driver's license and a car, he was looking for a job. He was also very happy to hear that in Russia, I had been driving for a few years. Only a few weeks later, I understood why Mark was so happy to meet a person who knew how to drive. We had spent over an hour talking, and I invited Mark to come over for dinner. Back at the apartment, I tried to remember everything Mark had told me, and I wrote down a lot of his advice in a notebook. The information I got from Mark was priceless.

When I told Sam about Mark, Sam and his family also showed up in the evening to meet him. Mark told us about his journey to Houston, how he'd gone from Russia to Israel, and how he made his journey to America after spending over a year in Israel. During that evening, he told us about job hunting and also that the most important step for us now would be buying a car.

I had to let my parents know that we were in America. Since there was no direct calling to Russia, I didn't know how to do it. Again, Mark helped me make that call; however, he warned me that it would be a very long process, mainly because the Russian operators were instructed to make it hard on us. I had to call AT&T and ask to be connected to Moscow. The Russian operators usually would answer only after the fifth attempt. The AT&T operators didn't speak Russian, and the Russians were saying that they didn't understand English. Since I was on the line and listening, I asked the Russian operator to connect me to my parents' phone in Beltsy. The Moscow operators couldn't call direct to my parents' home, they had to go through an operator in the capital of Moldova, Kishinev. Only on the third day of trying did an operator in Moscow call Kishinev. Then the operators in Kishinev told me that nobody was answering the phone at my parents' home. It was two a.m. in Beltsy, and it was impossible to believe that nobody would answer at that time. When I told that to the operator from Kishinev, she turned on a tape with prerecorded ringing, and after a few minutes, asked me before hanging up if I was satisfied with her efforts to make the connection.

After a few more days of trying, I finally got through and talked to my parents. It was a very emotional conversation, but we also knew that the KGB was taping our conversation, and we had to be very careful in choosing what we said to each other. We used our secret phrases during our telephone conversations. We knew that the KGB would simply cut off our conversations or destroy our letters should they feel that our communications were damaging the Soviet image. My parents were very happy to hear that we finally made it to America. We didn't talk in detail; just hearing each other's voices was great. There were tears on both sides, and when we had to say goodbye, the feelings were similar to those we had when leaving Russia.

Even though calling Russia was very expensive, I kept my promise to my parents by calling them at least twice a month. Calling from Russia was even harder, because in addition to the weekly waits, the calls from Russia were limited to three minutes, and the lines often went dead in the middle of our conversations. That was the way our communications went until the collapse of the Soviet Union.

Chapter 13

We were familiar with only a few products sold in the supermarkets, so we had to call our friends in Los Angeles and ask for their advice. Actually it was fun—our friends would spell the names of different foods for us to buy, we would take this list to the supermarket and show it to a clerk, who would take us to the shelves where the products were sold. We even worked out a system and checked off on our list only the products we liked so we would buy them again next time.

After a few weeks of being in Houston another JFS lady came to visit us. Her name was Donna, and she was assigned to help us with the job search. The fact that we were watching TV for almost ten hours daily and studying English every day enabled us to communicate a little.

Donna had a questionnaire for us to complete. The questions were written in both Russian and English. Donna also brought a sample of a resume and asked us to write our own resumes using this as an example. It didn't take long for us to complete the Russian part of the questionnaire, but when we tried to do it in English, it was a different story. I quickly realized that it wasn't so easy. My limited English vocabulary made it so hard that it took me almost a week to complete the questionnaire. As we were working on the questionnaire, we also tried to work on our resumes. I wrote my work experience in Russian and tried to translate it using the dictionary. Unfortunately, I had no idea that Russian and English sentences are structured completely differently, which made it very difficult for any American to understand exactly what we were trying to say. I realized that the resume I'd written was useless only when I saw the corrected one.

After we handed all of our paperwork back to Donna, she brought our resumes back to us in a few days, and they looked nothing like what we had written. She had combined our version with the answers from the questionnaires and wrote an English version of our resumes. We had no choice but to accept her version. It was also the time when I realized that no matter how hard I studied English, I wouldn't be able to explain my experience to a potential employer in a timely manner.

After a few days of unsuccessful preparation for an interview, I got an idea. Using a large piece of paper, I made a drawing of a pipe rack with pipes connecting pumps and storage tanks. I also wrote formulas showing supporting calculations for the pipes and nozzle sizes, as well as pipe supports. I felt much better when I did it, because I knew drawings and calculations were universally understood and were not dependent on fluent English.

In the early 1980s, Houston was the place to be if you wanted to find a job in the petrochemical industry. There were a few large companies, such as Bechtel, Fluor, Brown & Root, and Stone & Webster employing a large number of people, and for us it was the ultimate dream to land a job with one of them. However, we were advised not to seek an interview with any of the large companies. Instead, we were told to try at least ten interviews with smaller companies in order to gain the experience of a job interview.

On Monday mornings we made phone calls to the companies that were seeking engineers, designers, or drafters. It was extremely hard because we couldn't explain exactly what we wanted, nor could we understand the replies. A few times after hearing them answer the phone and not knowing what to say, I would simply hang up. Finally, I asked Donna to make a few phone calls for me. She actually scheduled a few appointments and even took us to the companies, but it didn't help us find jobs.

In order to get to the interviews by ourselves, we had to get driver's licenses and purchase a car. During our second week in Houston we decided it was time to do this. Mark told us how to get to the driver's license office, and early one morning, all of us headed over there. We quickly discovered that there were no sidewalks, and we found ourselves walking very close to fast-moving cars. We were forced to walk in the grassy areas and had no idea that walking wasn't a common way of commuting in Houston. At the driver's license office, we watched how the test was conducted, picked up a few test books, and went back to our apartments. Once back, we immediately began to study.

That same day after lunch, Robby began to complain about having throat pain, and by the evening he had developed a fever of 103. We had no medicine, and it was pretty scary. There was a small hospital about half a mile away from our apartments, and at eleven p.m. Sophia and I walked there with Robby. As we were trying to explain Robby's situation to the emergency personnel, the nurse, after checking his fever, quickly removed all of his clothes. Next she poured a bottle of rubbing alcohol on his body, waving a towel to create a breeze. Later we understood that this was done to cool his body temperature, but we were shocked at the time and didn't know what to do. Robby was crying very hard while the medical personnel were trying to explain that everything was okay and that we had to calm down. Only when we saw Robby's fever go down did we realize that this method worked. The nurse was trying to explain what we had to do when back at our apartment. We had very little understanding of what they were telling us, so after a few attempts they gave us medicine for Robby, wrote on a piece of paper the times for him to take it, and told us to go home.

We left the hospital without paying, and even now I don't know if they let us go without paying because we couldn't communicate or if they had a contract with the JFS and later billed them. The medicine they gave us worked, and after taking it for a few days, Robby was back to normal.

While we studied for the driver's license test, we checked the ads in the newspaper for used cars. Mark was our biggest help; he had already passed the driving test and had purchased a car. I didn't want to buy a large car. When I found a five-year-old small Chevy for sale, we decided to buy it. The car didn't have a lot of miles. Since we couldn't make it to the seller, Mark called, and the seller agreed to bring the car to us. We were very happy with that arrangement and didn't realize at the time that the seller was a used car dealer who would have done whatever it took to sell the car to us. In our eyes, the seller was simply a very nice man who understood our needs and was willing to help.

It happened that the car seller brought the car to us on the same day we all passed the driving test and got our driving permits. By having a permit and a passenger in the car who had a driver's license, I could actually legally drive a car on the streets. Mark sat with me to test drive the Chevy, and everything worked well. After a brief conversation with Sam regarding the car, the decision was made to buy it. The only problem was that the car's A/C wasn't working. The seller told us that he knew about this problem and assured me that all the A/C needed was a new belt. He promised that if I bought the car, he would

101

bring and install the belt in the morning. Somewhere in the back of my mind I knew that I would be better off paying him after he installed the belt, but my desire to drive my own car in the morning took over. After a short discussion with Sophia, I pulled out $1,500 we had saved from all our sales in Italy and handed it to the dealer. In return, he handed me a receipt, together with the title to the car. I had no idea that the title was the most important document in purchasing a car. After all the paperwork was completed, he told me that in the morning he'd be back to install the belt and left.

As soon as he left, we began to celebrate our second biggest achievement in America: we were car owners. In Russia, buying a car was almost impossible without one's parents' help, and if trying to do it the right way, it could take decades. Here, we'd done it within two weeks and without any help.

The next step for us was passing the driving test. I knew that it would be easy for Sam and me because both of us had driving experience. The very next morning, using my car, both of us, as expected, passed the driving test on our first try. Within an hour, we received our temporary licenses and officially became legal drivers in America. Without any fears, I drove my car back to our apartment. Shortly after Mark showed us how to use the map of Houston, I was ready to drive anywhere. Because of high speed, I was a little uneasy driving on the freeways, and for a week I avoided them. But within another week I had no more freeway fears, and it became my preferred way of driving.

In the evening, we decided to celebrate our biggest achievements in America. Sophia and Janet prepared a nice dinner, Sam and I bought a bottle of vodka, and we asked Mark to come over to celebrate with us. As the dinner progressed, all of us discovered that we weren't able to drink vodka the way we used to drink it in Russia. After the second shot we didn't feel like drinking anymore. It was almost unheard of, not only that we didn't want to drink but that we didn't have any desire. Looking back, I think this change happened because we felt much more responsibility. We couldn't afford to get drunk; we felt that our minds had to be clear at all times. Since Robby's fourth birthday was coming up, we also used this dinner to celebrate his birthday, the first one in America.

The next morning, I began the preparations for my phone calls to find employment. My drawing was also ready, and I thought that those two pieces together would help me find a job quickly.

Well, it didn't work out the way I anticipated. Because I used the dictionary in preparing my speech, the phone calls sounded like a bunch of words translated from Russian without any meaning for an English-speaking person. I was very afraid to make phone calls, however I called potential employers every day, just to practice. I also used the map to write down driving directions and drove to many companies just to drop off my resume and practice my driving. The first few weeks were very tough. I felt very uncomfortable and stupid, but I also knew that this was the only way for me to find a job.

Some employers didn't want to talk to me, however most were very friendly, trying very hard to understand me. I was reluctant to talk to any of them. I didn't know how to say what I wanted, and even worse, I couldn't understand their answers. I remember well how drained I felt after each of those conversations. I had to recover after each conversation by sitting in my car for a few minutes before going on to the next company. Usually I was back in the apartment by three p.m., and after a short break, I would teach Sophia how to drive a car.

In April we began to feel the effect of the nonworking A/C in our car. The car dealer had never come back to install the belt, nor did he ever return any of the calls we made. When the weather became hotter, I bought and installed the belt. It didn't help; the A/C still didn't work. We had to purchase a new compressor, but we didn't have the money to buy it. For the interviews, I wore a suit, and Sophia had long-sleeved dresses, and we were hot and sweaty. Suddenly, more car problems began to appear. Often after stopping at intersections, the car would stop running. Every time it happened, I had to get out of the car, unplug the alternator wires, plug them back in, and hope it would start. Quite a few times strangers would stop, helping me push the car to a parking lot.

As we got more involved with our job search, the Jewish Federation helped us by taking care of Robby as well as Sam's kids. They enrolled them in the preschool at the Jewish Community Center. We didn't have to pay, and our kids, in addition to being in very good hands, were together with other kids their age. Every day they were getting more and more comfortable there and were learning more English words. Very soon, Robby was watching TV programs and explaining what he was watching. Taking good care of our kids was one of the most important things the Federation did for us. It was such a great relief not to worry about them during the day. It allowed us to do what we had to do—concentrate on our job search.

Chapter 14

I remember well the day when Mark told me that he had been hired by S&B Engineering as a piping drafter with a salary of $12 per hour. It was great news for all of us; we all were encouraged by his success. Mark was very happy but also very nervous. He didn't have any piping experience and had no idea what he would be asked to do. On the day Mark started his job he told his boss about me, and I was called for an interview the very next day. After a short interview and a look at my drawing, I was offered a drafting position with the pay of $12 per hour as well. This was like a dream come true—I couldn't believe it!

The following morning I began working in America, making a lot of money. Sophia and I were extremely happy, still thinking that this was a dream. Mark and I were happy not just that we found jobs, but also because we would be able to drive together and help each other during the day. The night before I had to start, Mark told me that he was asked to make an isometric piping drawing and had been working on it during the day and making very good progress.

After a sleepless night, I drove to the office and arrived there much earlier than requested. At exactly eight a.m., I entered the office and was directed to the personnel department to complete my paperwork. I quickly realized that I didn't know how to answer most of the questions on the application. Finally, around lunchtime, we were done with the paperwork, and I was shown to my work desk. I didn't know what I was expected to do, and as I sat down at my desk, Mark showed up. Seeing him was a great relief for me, as I was counting on Mark to know all of the answers. It didn't take long for me to realize that this wasn't the case.

Mark asked me to look at the drawing he had been working on for the past two days, and I couldn't believe what I saw. It was a drawing of a pipe rack supporting six pipes. Mark, as a mechanical engineer, made an isometric drawing the way it was done in mechanical engineering, where all details were in three dimensions. I knew, based on my piping experience, that the word isometric meant something completely different—the pipes and the rack had to be shown in a single line. When I asked Mark if he was told to make an isometric drawing the way he was doing it, he answered that all he was told was to do an isometric drawing from a sketch. While I was trying to explain to him that this was not the way piping drawings were done, I began to think that this might be the way it's done in America. Regardless, I made a decision that if asked, I would do the drawing the way I knew how to make it. To my surprise, instead of getting a sketch, I was given a book with the specifications to read. That was very hard; I had to use my dictionary for almost every word. I took it home with me and for the entire evening, Sophia and I worked on translating it and making notes.

The second day was very similar to the first; no work was given to me. It was only when I was ready to go home that one of the designers brought me a sketch and asked me to start the drawing in the morning. I took the sketch home, trying to translate all the notes and getting ready to work on the drawing first thing in the morning. I had also prepared a list of questions for the designer. He was trying very hard to explain his answers, and I was doing my best to understand exactly what he was saying. Based on my experience, I knew that before making the drawing I would need to make calculations and make sure that everything worked as designed. I spent most of the day doing that. I didn't know that this was not my job and all I had to do was make the drawing from the sketch.

On the way home, Mark told me that his drawing was ready and that he was planning to turn it in to his boss first thing in the morning. I was planning to wait and see what they told Mark before starting my drawing. I took my calculations to the designer, and he was very surprised to see them but was even more surprised and confused when I asked him to look at Mark's drawing. All I wanted to know was whether this was the way my drawing should be done. On the way back to my desk, the designer showed me a drawing and told me how the drawings should look at their final stage. It was the way I was planning to do it, not the way Mark had done it.

For the first time since I started my job, I felt good about what I was doing. I knew that it wouldn't take me more than a day to finish the drawing, and I immediately began to work on it. I was happy to see the person who offered me this job when he showed up at my desk before lunchtime. He asked me to follow him to his office. I was surprised to see Mark there. As soon as he closed the door, we were told that unfortunately, they had to let us go. He said that it was not because our piping knowledge was lacking, but rather it was because of our language barrier. He told us to learn English first and then come back. He even told us that he'd hire us back after we learned English. He then gave each of us an envelope and told us that we were free to go home. I still wasn't sure what exactly had happened and kept asking when I should come back and finish my drawing. Finally, he made it very clear that we were fired and no longer had a job there. After realizing what had happened I felt terrible, but somehow, I didn't feel as bad as I would have expected. I knew that I had done the best I could, and even before we left the office I was already thinking of the immediate steps I should take: learn English, start the job search again, and improve our driving conditions by fixing the car.

When we got in the car, Mark and I opened the envelopes and couldn't believe our eyes. My check was in the amount of four hundred and eighty dollars, which was a huge amount of money for us. They paid me for a whole week, even though I had only worked there for three days. Mark also was very happy. They paid him for two weeks of work, and his check was in the amount of nine hundred and sixty dollars. Although it was hard for me to tell Sophia that I lost my job, both of us came to the conclusion that we were rich, and the money I received would give us a chance to study English longer, enabling us to find better jobs.

However, in the evening I began to worry again about my ability to find a new job in a timely manner. I even thought about looking for a non-engineering job just to make money until I found a job in my field. But in the morning I reconsidered this idea and decided to use all of my energy and efforts to find an engineering job. I knew that I'd lost my job not only because of my poor English, but also because I hadn't had the chance to show my knowledge.

The very next day I went to four companies, but none of them were even interested in talking to me. None of those companies were from the list of the most desirable companies, however. So I decided that for the next week I'd pick a few good companies that were looking for petrochemical drafters, designers, or engineers and would try to get an appointment with them.

Sunday's newspaper had a few ads from large companies such as Bechtel, Brown & Root, etc. that were looking for experienced people. There were also ads from a few mid-size companies, and those were the first on my list to be contacted. I made my first call on Monday morning to a company called DM International. It was a British-based company with an office in Houston. I was pretty sure that I'd hear the same answer I had heard over and over during the past week—that the position was not available anymore. However, when I was asked to come in for an interview, I was so shocked that I forgot to ask when they wanted me there.

Sophia and I became very excited; it was unheard of to be invited for an interview after the first call. We decided not to waste any time. I dressed up and went to the company right away. It was a short drive from our apartment, so when I showed up there in less than two hours, the personnel manager was very impressed and asked me to complete the necessary applications. It was very hard to understand and answer most of the questions—I had to use the dictionary a lot—but after an hour and a half, I turned in the applications to the receptionist.

After a short wait, the personnel manager asked me to follow him to his office. He told me that he was not the technical person I would need to talk to regarding my engineering knowledge. He explained that his job was to learn more about my previous employment, salary, etc. I was trying very hard to understand him, and finally, I asked if he could speak slower, even though I knew from other Russians that this request could work against me. To my surprise he smiled, and in addition to slowing down, he also tried to use pen and paper to make sure I understood him. When I couldn't understand him even after he repeated the question a few times, he would spell the word for me, and a few times I actually had to use the dictionary. With all of this help, we were able to communicate. Most of the questions were related to the reasons we had left Russia, how we did it, and if we had any family or friends here in Houston. He had only one question regarding the job I was applying for—he wanted to know if I knew the position title I was applying for. His reason for asking was because on my resume he saw that I had an MSME, but the opening they had was for a drafter. I remember my answer well: "It doesn't matter to me, I can do everything you would like me to do."

After getting all the information he walked with me to the waiting area, telling me to wait for the engineering manager. I really didn't understand what I had to do at that point and was thinking that I was done with the interview. I was almost ready to leave, thinking that they'd call for another interview with the engineering manager. I knew they couldn't make the hiring decision just based on my conversation with the personnel manager. My hope of getting a job was based strictly on the drawing I had made, and I didn't even have a chance to show it.

I was so preoccupied with those thoughts that when the receptionist asked me a question, I answered "thank you" without understanding what she'd said. She smiled, and by the time I was ready to leave, she handed me a cup of coffee, saying that someone from the engineering department would be with me soon. Shortly after I took my first sip, a man showed up, shook my hand, and asked me to follow him.

When we got to his office, I decided to tell him that it would help me a great deal if he could speak slowly. He smiled, telling me that the personnel manager had already warned him and assured me that he didn't mind taking the time to talk slowly. I also decided to make the first move. I opened my briefcase, pulled out my drawing together with the supporting calculations, and handed it to him. As I was showing him my drawing, I began my supporting speech that I'd memorized. I said, "Since I do not speak good

English, I have made a sample of work I was doing in Russia." I was afraid that he would not even look at the drawing. He seemed to be puzzled for a moment, but when he looked at the drawing and the calculations, his facial expression made me believe that my strategy could be working.

He spent a few minutes reviewing my drawing and the calculations, and then asked me if this was typical engineering work in Russia. After I assured him that it was, he explained to me that this was the job of an engineer, a designer, and a draftsman here in the USA. He asked me a few questions related to the drawing, asked me to make a quick sketch to make sure I knew what I was doing, and invited me to join him and the piping engineering manager for lunch. I agreed without any idea what I was doing. I was also very concerned about the amount of money the lunch would cost. All three of us went to a nearby Hilton hotel where they were serving a lunch buffet. Since I couldn't understand most of the menu items, I was looking at the prices and realized that there were only a few items on the menu in my price range. When the people who invited me to lunch understood that I was trying to find inexpensive food, they told me not to worry about the cost because lunch was on them. I understood what they told me and felt great relief. I placed some food on my plate without knowing what it was.

The piping manager was asking me questions and was trying very hard to understand me. Sometimes he even used napkins to write and spell some words, and a few times I had to pull out the dictionary in order to understand or answer questions. After a few engineering questions, they switched the conversation from engineering to my personal life. They wanted to know my reasons for leaving Russia and asked questions about my

111

family as well as the country I had left. Since most of my English vocabulary was work-related, it was very hard for me to keep up the conversation. They wanted to know about my hobbies, and since the word hobby in English has the same meaning that it has in Russian, I decided to impress them and answered that fishing was my hobby. I used fishing because it was one of the very few English words I knew. Very soon I realized that I had made a mistake, because both of them were avid fishermen. They were asking me questions about fishing in Russia and telling me about fishing in Houston. It was pretty much a one-way conversation.

When leaving the restaurant, I realized that I hadn't touched my food. Back in his office, the engineering manager thanked me for coming in and told me that Mr. Zachariah would call me in a few days. When I made it home I was so tired that all I could do was remove my suit and lie down. Sophia was eager to hear my story, but all I could tell her was that everything had gone well before I fell asleep.

After I woke up Sophia and I analyzed each step of my interview and were trying to determine if everything I had done over there was good enough to get a job offer. The conclusion we came up with was that, most likely, I wouldn't get the job because I wasn't even asked about the terms and the money. Neither Sophia nor I were upset with that; I felt that this kind of experience would help me land a job in the future.

The next morning, just as I was ready to make my phone calls, the telephone rang. Both Sophia and I hated to answer the phone. Talking over the phone was a big challenge for us because we couldn't see the person's lips and had to rely only on what we heard. After looking at each other for a few seconds, I finally answered the phone.

It was the personnel manager who had interviewed me the day before. He spoke very slowly, telling me that his company was prepared to make me an offer to work for them as a draftsman. I couldn't believe what I was hearing, and to make sure I understood correctly what he was telling me, I loudly repeated every word for Sophia to hear it as well. She understood and gave me the okay sign, confirming that I had received a job offer. Sophia was all smiles; it felt great until he began talking again. I couldn't understand him; the only word I could hear was the word sorry. My first reaction was that he changed his mind about the offer. After a while, without hearing a response from me, he realized that he had spoken too fast. Very slowly, he repeated his sentence, while I echoed every word for Sophia to hear.

Only then did I understand that they were sorry for not offering me an engineering position due to my poor English, and the best they could do at that time was to offer me a draftsman's position. He couldn't know that I would have accepted any offer; the title didn't matter to me. All I wanted was to get a job and to be able to support my family.

After answering that his offer was okay with me, he told me that my starting salary would be $11 per hour, plus time and a half for overtime. He was also trying to explain that, as a bonus to all hourly employees, the company offered a forty-five hour workweek, meaning that I would automatically have five hours of overtime every week. The offer was too good to be true; it was much more than I had expected. I wanted to jump and scream *yes, yes, yes I accept it*! Instead of doing that, I thanked him and asked if I could call him back. As soon as I hung up, Sophia and I looked at each other, trying to understand why I hadn't answered yes. Immediately all of my happy feelings were overtaken by the fear that not accepting it right away could jeopardize their offer.

I couldn't wait any longer, and after a two-hour wait, I called them back to accept the offer. I was afraid that they would change their minds, so when the personnel manager told me that he was happy about my decision to accept the offer, it was a great relief for both Sophia and me. When I told him that I'd be there in the morning, he sounded a little surprised, but answered, "Of course." I didn't know it was uncommon to start the job the day after receiving an offer. I couldn't sleep that night. I was thinking about how to avoid any mistakes on my first day. I was afraid to end up in a situation similar to that of my first job a few weeks prior.

In the morning, I expected to begin my drafting work right after the paperwork in the personnel office was finished. Instead, the personnel manager walked me to my desk and brought a lot more forms for me to complete. He knew that it would take a long time for me to do that, so with a smile he told me not to rush, that I had the whole day to do it. I was working very hard filling out the forms, when suddenly one by one, people who were working in the same room began coming over to introduce themselves and to welcome me as their newest co-worker. They were smiling, talking to me, and asking questions. It was overwhelming; I didn't expect anything like that. Even though most of their questions went unanswered, and I couldn't understand most of the conversations, they made me feel good. It was five minutes past five p.m. when I looked at the clock. It was time to go home, but I was afraid to leave. I left my desk only after one of the drafters came over to tell me it was time to go home.

The next morning, I was invited to the office of the engineering manager. He congratulated me on getting the job, telling me that he was happy about my decision to accept the drafter's position. He introduced me to a designer and told me that, in addition to giving me work assignments, he had asked the designer to teach me nonwork-related issues as well. A few months later, the manager explained to me that after seeing me at lunch, he realized that I needed much more than just knowledge of the English language. He chose a very nice man to be my mentor, as well as my immediate supervisor.

Later in the day I was given the company's engineering manual. As I looked through the pages, I realized that piping isometrics in the USA were made the same way as in Russia. That was a very big relief for me. The formulas in the manuals were very familiar to me, and that made me feel even better. I knew that if I was given the opportunity, I would be able to keep my job and do it very well. Almost every day I was discovering new items I didn't know existed. For example, I didn't know about electrical erasers, mechanical pencils, and pocket calculators. After seeing me use a regular eraser, my designer showed me his electrical eraser. The next week I bought one for myself. The same happened with calculators; I was using paper and the logogriph ruler for my calculations. He told me where to buy a calculator and spent a good amount of time teaching me how to use it. After getting the eraser, and especially mechanical pencils, I made my drawings so fast that the designer told me a few times to slow down. I was making the drawings faster than he could do the calculations, and pretty soon we were doing calculations together. Quickly I began gaining respect not only from him, but also from others, including the piping manager.

Chapter 15

Datsun 210 - our first car
Robby, Sophia, me

As I was working away, Sophia had intensified her job search, and within a few weeks she found a job as a drafter in a small civil engineering firm with a starting salary of $7 per hour. People working there were quite nice, guiding her through her very rough first weeks. And it wasn't just work-related issues they were helping her with—her boss bought a vacuum cleaner for us after learning that we had to borrow one from the apartment office. Almost every day Sophia and I practiced driving, and soon thereafter, she successfully passed the driving test and received her driver's license.

We saved money from every paycheck, our savings account was growing, and we were thinking of buying a second car. In the meantime, we shared one car. I was dropping off Sophia well before she had to be at her job in order to make it on time to my job. Even though the Jewish Federation helped us with Robby by placing him in the preschool at the Jewish Community Center, we were still facing a problem. I had to drop off Sophia at six-thirty in the morning, but the school only opened at seven. The solution we found was to take Robby over to Sam's apartment while he was still asleep, and they could take him together with their kids to the JCC. Robby was at JCC until six in the evening; it was the earliest we could pick him up on the way home.

At my job I was doing most of the designer's work in addition to drafting, and within three months of starting the job, I was promoted to a designer's position. This promotion came with a dollar-per-hour salary increase and a terrible scare for me. I remember this day well. It was a Friday when the engineering manager stopped at my desk and asked me to step into his office. It didn't sound good—everyone knew that if there were layoffs, the management would notify employees on Friday by calling people to their offices. As I was following the manager to his office, I was sure that this was my last day of work, and I was trying hard to understand why I would be let go. It looked like they were pleased with the work I was doing; at least everyone was telling me so. I knew it couldn't be my work. The only reason I could think of was my poor English. During that short walk to the manager's office I even began planning to take English classes before finding another job. I knew it would be very beneficial for my future employment.

Since Sophia began working, we had saved almost $7,000, so I could afford being temporarily unemployed while studying. As we entered the manager's office, I was so preoccupied with my planning that I hadn't noticed his smiling face and his offer to have a cup of coffee with him. I was ready to get my final paycheck and go home. When he looked at me he suddenly realized how scared I was. Immediately he told me that I was not losing my job, but rather, he was promoting me to the designer's position. He came over, shook my hand and told me that when my English improved, he would be happy to promote me to an engineering position.

All that was so overwhelming—within a few minutes my mind went from the fear of losing my job to the happiness of being promoted, getting more money, and getting a promise to be promoted to an engineering position. When I returned to my desk, I couldn't help but take a break to cool off. My co-workers were aware of my promotion, and they were happy for me and congratulated me. For the first time in America I felt that I had job security. My promotion at work, a sizable amount in our savings account, and Sophia's job made me think while driving home in a car without air conditioning that it was time for us to purchase a new car. At home we celebrated my promotion, and Sophia agreed that the time was right for us to buy a new car.

We were looking for a small car, and with the help of a friend who worked as a mechanic at a Nissan dealership, we purchased a brand new Datsun B210 station wagon. There was an option to buy it with or without an air conditioner. The price difference was $500, and our friend convinced me to buy it without the air conditioner. The plan was for him to purchase the A/C unit at the employees' discount price, and with my help, install it over the weekend. A few days later, Sophia, Robby, and I drove our brand new car home from the dealership. There was a lot of excitement in our family; we were celebrating the biggest purchase we had ever made in our lives, and it felt very good.

As planned, our friend and I installed the air conditioner; however, there were problems with the installation. The problems never went away. Every few months, I had to take the car to the dealership for A/C repairs. Since they didn't install the A/C I didn't have a warranty and had to pay for the repairs. By the time I sold my car, the A/C repair expenses were much greater than the original savings of $500. It was a costly mistake, but we'd learned a very important lesson in this country.

After driving Sophia to her job for almost three months, we also decided it was time for us to buy another car. Since Sophia didn't have a lot of driving experience, we decided to buy a large American car for safety reasons. After a short search, we purchased a five-year-old Chevrolet Malibu Classic. It was a very large eight-cylinder car, and it had a very nice ride. The only problem was that it needed a lot of gasoline, so we used it only as a method of transportation to Sophia's job.

Sophia was getting very comfortable at her job, also doing much more than a regular drafter would be doing. We knew she could make more money doing the same work at a larger company. After working for six months at the small firm, Sophia mailed out her resumes to all the large companies in Houston, and shortly after being interviewed, she received an offer from Brown & Root. In addition to getting a better job and better benefits, she also got a healthy increase in her salary. Between the two of us, we were making over $25.00 per hour. That was a lot of money back in 1981. Even with our new car payment, every paycheck we were able to save a sizable amount of money, and our savings account was growing.

Our friends and co-workers encouraged us to buy a house for various reasons, and the most important one was to avoid paying back in taxes almost twenty percent of our earnings. All that was new to us, but we decided to follow their advice. We set a goal to save $15,000 before looking for a house. With our expenses being very minimal, we saved not only our overtime earnings, but also a portion of our regular salary, and we got closer to our goal quickly.

As we became more and more comfortable with our life in America, we began our learning journey of new products available at the grocery store, and every time we went grocery shopping we would buy one new product to try. It was fun, in most cases we had no idea what we were buying, and quite often we would end up throwing away the new product. We also developed another tradition— every time we bought groceries we would visit the toy department and let Robby pick a toy. We were probably as happy as Robby was because we finally could afford to purchase toys for our child. I remember well that one of his very first choices was a doctor's kit with a stethoscope. He wore it around his neck in our apartment, asking to check everyone.

Everything was going well for us. Our English was improving, allowing us to understand and enjoy more and more things in America. Yes, our English was much better than a year ago, but way far from the level we could feel comfortable. As a result of my poor English, a very unforgettable episode happened while I was at work at DMI. Around 4pm I received a phone call from Sophia's coworker telling me that she took Sophia to the hospital. She was trying to calm me down, explain that Sophia didn't feel well and passed out. At that time I didn't know that passed out and passed away had different meanings. I understood that my wife died. Without telling anyone, I jumped in to my car, and was at the hospital within a few minutes. I was in stage of a shock, ready to see my wife's body, not understanding how and why it happened. At the entrance to the hospital, Sophia's coworker was waiting for me. Later she told me that my look really puzzled her, I was a total crying mess. She had no clue about my thoughts of Sophia being dead. At the same time I couldn't understand why is she all smiles. She showed me the way to the ER, and over there I saw Sophia sitting in a chair, waiving at me. I don't remember exactly what happened during the next few seconds. I do remember hugging Sophia, and telling her what I was expecting to find when coming in to the ER. Everyone in the room had a very good laugh. Sophia and I didn't laugh, it took a week for me to recover from this.

As we were settling in, we began to relax more, which also allowed me to start thinking more about my parents and sister. Whenever we talked, I got the feeling that they were not doing well over there. My dad's health was declining, he had to be taken to the hospital more often, and there were not many options available over there to help him. My hope to quickly bring them to America was also diminishing. In addition to the government making it even harder for people like them to leave, my sister's husband had changed his mind and decided not to leave Russia. This prevented my parents and sister from applying for their exit visas. My sister had to divorce and get his permission to leave Russia before she could even apply. When she finally got divorced, together with my parents she applied for their exit visas. The year was 1982 and they were one of the last people who were allowed to apply. Soon thereafter, the Russians stopped accepting exit visas.

Time passed without any results. I felt helpless and didn't know how to assist my parents. Sophia was my biggest help in staying focused on the positive side of this situation. She kept telling me that by the time my parents arrived, we'd be in a much better situation to help them, and they wouldn't have to experience nearly as many difficulties as we had upon our arrival. Her strategy worked, and between long working hours and regular phone calls to my parents, I overcame these fears and concentrated on improving our preparedness for my parents' arrival.

Our work situation was quite good, and we knew that the only way for our life to get better was to learn more English. Our jobs provided the most exposure to the language, with the second biggest source of exposure being our TV. We were still using the same 13-inch black-and-white television set given to us upon arrival. The quality was very poor. One evening after returning from his friend's house, Robby started a conversation about a nice TV they had; that was when Sophia and I decided it was time for us to purchase a new color TV set. In Russia, we had heard about the Sony brand, and that's what we decided to buy. We purchased a 27-inch TV set; it was very large, heavy, and beautiful. It took Sam, Mark, Mark's friend, and me to move it to our second-floor apartment. The quality of the picture was amazing. We paid over $1,000 for the TV set, and it became the second most significant purchase for us. Some of the Russians, after seeing our new purchase, told us that we were crazy for spending so much money. We had no regrets because watching more TV tremendously improved our English. The TV set also lasted for a very long time—we used it for nine years, gave it to my mom and sister when they arrived, and three years later, they passed it on to their friends who had just arrived from Russia. In all those years, it had never been repaired, and the picture quality was always great.

At work, both Sophia and I made it very clear that we would work all available overtime, and quite often, I worked seven days a week. We were saving money, and by the end of the year, we had almost reached our goal of $15,000. When we were first advised to buy a house, we hadn't seriously considered it. After completing our first 1040 form we quickly reconsidered. We decided to move ahead with purchasing a house after realizing that almost a quarter of our savings would have to be returned back to the government. We were very puzzled by the fact that most Russian families who arrived prior to us were still living in an apartment. We couldn't understand their reasons for not buying a house, but we decided to buy one anyway.

Chapter 16

We learned an important lesson at this time in our lives: Russian immigrants were not ready to discuss their personal lives, and especially give advice. Since we had no knowledge of this, we totally relied on the advice given to us by a Russian immigrant who became a real estate broker. We were so naïve, totally trusting and hoping that because of our similar backgrounds he would make sure we wouldn't make any mistakes while buying our first house. We had no idea that he was getting commissions from the seller. As a matter of fact, we didn't even know about brokers making commissions from their sales.

After finding a house, he made us believe that he was on our side during the negotiations with the owner. At the same time, the broker also tried to convince us that we should make an offer slightly higher than the asking price in order for the seller to even look at our offer. He also made us believe that it was not customary in the US to negotiate when you buy a house. Lastly, he made a recommendation that we use all of our money as a down payment.

Looking back, we see that he did all of this strictly for his own benefit. Only later, when we sold the house, did we realize how poorly the transaction was handled; we couldn't even sell the house without the previous seller's approval. Fortunately for us, the seller was a Jewish person who we'd gotten to know through a mutual friend, and none of the issues we had accepted by signing the contract were used against us. It was also at that time when we discovered that the seller was ready to sell his house at a reduced price, but the Russian broker told him about our willingness to pay the asking price. Within a month we were approved to buy the house and got the mortgage. By the time we paid our down payment, we didn't have any money left to buy furniture, window treatments, etc.

We didn't have a lot of possessions, so it took us less than a day to move in. We had very mixed feelings. While we were proud to have our own house, we were also worried that we had lost all of our savings. It was the same feeling we had when we'd first arrived in America; we had no financial security anymore. We tried our best to enjoy our empty house, and quite often we questioned whether we had made the right decision.

However, we had to move forward, so after we received our next paycheck we bought window treatments. We had to do it in order to replace the tablecloth we were using as a curtain. Slowly we began to make other small purchases, and soon our house became quite livable. Robby was very happy because we had a big backyard with some large trees. He made friends and, together with Sam's kids, they spent a lot of time playing in the backyard. I also enjoyed the backyard until I realized that the grass was growing fast. Within ten days of moving in, I had to cut the grass. My co-workers helped me buy a used lawn mower; one of them even came over on the weekend to give me a lesson on grass mowing. It took over three hours for me to mow our front and backyards, and it didn't help when I saw a snake next to me. The snake scared me so badly that I left the mower running and ran to the house. When I told my friends at work about the snake, they all laughed and advised me to buy a pair of Texas boots.

Buying boots sounded very appealing; in addition to the protection I would get, I could also send a photo to my parents of myself wearing Texas boots. For most people in Russia, Texas was only associated with cowboys, and for my parents and friends to see me in a pair of cowboy boots would mean that I had truly become one of the Texans. Adapting to the new country was one of the many words of advice my parents had given us when we were leaving Russia, and I knew they would be very happy seeing me dressed as a cowboy.

To our surprise, buying the house also helped us to decrease the number of our new Russian friends. When all of us were living in the apartments, most of them were friendly. That drastically changed when we purchased our house and moved away from the apartments. Most of the Russians couldn't accept the fact that Sophia and I, two of the youngest people who'd come to America after them, had moved to a house while they were still staying at the same apartment complex. We saw it first at our housewarming party a few weeks after we moved in. Our American friends were happy for us, giving us well-wishes, tips, and housewarming gifts. In contrast, most of our Russian friends were jealous and tried to put us down, telling us how hard it would become for us to make monthly payments, that we would have to work much harder without saving any money, etc. It wasn't easy, but at that point we had no choice but to cut ties with the majority of the Russian community.

Another example of the Russians' jealousy happened on a hot Sunday afternoon when I was cutting the grass. A Russian couple showed up uninvited and asked if we could have a shot of cognac and grill some meat together. It was common for them to show up at our place because they couldn't grill at the apartments and didn't have the money to buy cognac. When I answered that now wasn't a good time for a drink, he replied that if I showed him where the cognac was stored, he and his wife would enjoy it while I continued to cut the grass. Both of them told me that we had made a mistake buying the house because I had to take care of the house rather than enjoying life, as they were doing. That was the last straw for me.

I lost my patience and asked them to leave my house.

At work, Sophia and I were getting more comfortable with our responsibilities. We worked very hard to get back to our financial comfort zone, but there was a significant drawback to doing this. As a family, we weren't spending enough time together. Robby was spending most of his days at JCC while Sophia and I were at work. On the rare occasion that we had a day off, all of us would drive to the JCC's camp in Rosenberg, about thirty miles from Houston. It was a great place to relax, and we grilled, swam, and played tennis there. I bought two Jack Kramer wooden tennis rackets so Robby and I could play every time we were there. I had never played tennis in Russia and didn't know the rules, but Robby liked it very much, and I enjoyed every moment of it. This initial experience, I believe, gave Robby the base to become a very good tennis player later in his life. After realizing that we had to do more family activities together, we cut our overtime weekend work, and that helped us a lot.

In November of 1982 Sophia and I decided to visit her parents. It was our first trip ever since we had arrived in America, and we spent two weeks in Israel. The first week we spent with Sophia's parents. During the second week, Sophia's cousins took us all over the country, from Kiryat Shmona in the north to the resort of Eilat in the south. Even though it was a very expensive trip, we felt good about our decision to visit Israel and see firsthand the place we could always make our home.

By the time the Moscow Olympic Games were over, and Russia didn't need any more American wheat, the Russians stopped allowing people to emigrate. My parents received an answer from the KGB that their request to leave Russia had been denied. The official reason they were given was that the Russian government didn't see any need for our families to reunite. This was a very hard blow to my parents, especially for my dad. He was hoping to achieve his biggest dream: to make sure my sister and I were together. His health was quickly deteriorating, he had to be admitted to the hospital almost every two weeks and couldn't work anymore. In addition to his health problems, my parents and sister had to be extremely cautious in everything they were doing because at that point, they were also considered traitors. My dad, who always knew how to deal with the authorities, couldn't do it anymore because of his poor health. I felt terrible and helpless; I didn't know how to help them.

In the midst of all that, at the beginning of 1983, the oil boom had slowed down, and so did the economy in Houston, which directly correlated with oil production. With oil prices dropping, a lot of oil companies canceled refinery construction, leaving design and construction companies in Houston without work. It was a bad situation, and every day over a thousand employees in Houston were given pink slips. Sophia lost her Brown & Root job in the beginning of February. This was a very hard blow to our stability and to the comfort we had been enjoying for the last year. I knew that eventually I would also lose my job unless new orders came in. The work I was doing had been scheduled for completion within two or three months, and with no new projects coming, it was just a matter of time before I would be unemployed as well.

Sophia and I decided to be proactive and try to reduce our monetary obligations before both of us were unemployed. We couldn't get rid of the car payment since we had to have a reliable source of transportation, so the decision was to sell our house. Selling a house in Houston was not an easy task. With so many people losing their jobs, there were thousands of homes for sale. After talking to a real estate agent, we realized that we had no chance of selling our house for a price that would even cover our mortgage. A lot of people were walking away from their homes, and some streets had more empty homes than occupied. We didn't want to walk away from the house, but we also didn't want to lose money on the closing.

One day while driving home, we saw a For Sale sign by a builder, who was trying to sell his brand new houses. His houses were within a mile of our home, they were smaller and priced lower than our house was. Sophia and I came up with the idea of trading our house for one of his new ones. We offered to buy his $90,000 brand new house with a 5% down payment if he would pay us $10,000 and take over payments for our house, which was valued at around $140,000. To our surprise, he agreed. That was when we found out about our contract's provision to obtain the previous owner's permission and approval for the buyer. Without knowing it, when buying our house, we had agreed that the previous owner would have to approve the buyer if we decided to sell the house.

At the closing, we were offered an option to purchase layoff insurance, which we did. The terms were that for an extra $20 a month, should I lose my job during the first two years from the house purchase, our mortgage payment, including taxes, would be covered for a period of six months. Within two weeks we moved into our new house. It was a very nice house, and our furniture filled it very well.

Sophia was unsuccessful in finding a new job, and at my company every week people were let go. When I asked my manager why more experienced engineers had been let go before me, he told me that my salary and the work I did were the reasons. I have since discovered how underpaid I was in comparison to others. Finally, at the end of March, I was told that there was nothing else for me to do, and I lost my job.

It was a very bad day in my life, because I lost control of our financial independence and knew that there was no chance of finding a new job within a reasonable amount of time. The next morning, I realized that it wasn't all that bad. I received a three-week severance paycheck, the unemployment benefits at that time were extended to nine months, and most importantly, my unemployment mortgage benefits would start immediately. That was a huge relief because for the next six months, we wouldn't have to worry about mortgage payments, which totaled over sixteen hundred dollars a month.

Chapter 17

Sophia and I worked very hard to find job opportunities. We sent out dozens of resumes and called every engineering company listed in the Yellow Pages. Even with all our efforts, we couldn't even get a job interview. Sophia and I even made a pledge to find jobs by using the local TV. The local CBS TV station was trying to help unemployed people find jobs, so every evening during prime time they allowed two job seekers to read their resumes. One day while I was in line at the unemployment office, a CBS representative approached me and offered me this opportunity. I was told to prepare a minute-and-a-half speech about my work experience and read it in front of the camera at their studio. When I arrived at the studio and was getting ready to pre-record my speech, I was told that nothing was going to be recorded and that I would be on live TV. That was pretty scary, and all I remember was a lot of lights in front of me. At home, Sophia taped my speech, so we had the opportunity to watch it many times. In our opinion I did very well, finishing my statement with a pledge of my willingness to relocate anywhere in the world if there was a job opportunity. I was expecting a lot of phone calls the next morning, but to our major disappointment, only two potential employers called.

Later we discovered the main reason for such a poor response: it was Oscars night, and not too many people chose to watch me over the Oscars. While at the TV studio, I had asked if Sophia could also appear on their station to try to find a job. A week later, Sophia made her pitch on live TV and received six phone calls. Unfortunately, none of the calls turned into job offers.

Every day, in addition to sending my resume all over the country, I drove to different local companies in Houston, dropping off my resume and trying to convince the receptionists to allow me to be interviewed. Most times it didn't work.

After losing my job, I spoke to my parents only once; I really didn't want them to know about our job situation and worry about us. During this call, my dad was unusually emotional. I could hear sadness in his voice as he was telling me that he was okay in response to my question about his health. I didn't like that and tried to assure him that soon we'd be able to see each other here, that we had extra rooms in our house, so they would be staying with us. His answer was that there were no doubts in his mind about us seeing each other soon, but he said that he was very troubled that my sister and I were so far away from each other. I didn't have a good feeling about my dad's health or his state of mind after hanging up.

Unfortunately, that was my last conversation with my dad. On May 2, 1983, around nine a.m., the phone rang. It was my mom telling me that Dad passed away on April 28th and was buried the next day. He would have turned sixty-one two weeks later, on May 10th. I don't remember much of our conversation; I remember sitting on the floor holding onto the wall, and I also remember my sister's voice telling me the details of our father's death. Finally the Russian operator told us that the conversation was over. I wanted to talk to my mom again and begged the operator not to disconnect us. But with pleasure in her voice, she answered that that was all she could do for traitors like me and cut the line. I was home alone, couldn't get in touch with Sophia, and had to get out of the house. The next thing I remember was sitting in a bar having a drink. Even now I don't remember how I drove to the bar. Sophia and Robby were home when I made it back, and as I told them about my dad. I remember having more drinks, trying to get drunk. In addition to being very sad, I also felt helpless. I knew that my mom and Polina could use my help, but there was nothing I could do from here to help them. I couldn't even call them; the Russians wouldn't connect me, even though the AT&T operators kept trying, as I told them it was an emergency call and that there was a death in the family.

Finally, a few days later, I got through the Russian operators and talked to my mom. When I asked why they had waited to inform me about Dad's death, my mom answered that the Russians hadn't let the call to go through despite knowing that there was a death in the family. I remember how hard it was for me to understand why the Russians made it so difficult for us to talk. Our two years of life in a free society had changed my way of thinking.

For the next few weeks I didn't do a lot. I stopped my job search, had more drinks than I needed, and didn't sleep much. The TV and cognac became my best friends.

One day I woke up realizing that this couldn't continue for much longer and that I shouldn't expect help from people just because they felt sorry for me. I realized that I was the one who needed to find a job, that I was the one who had to provide a roof and food for my own family. This became a breaking point. That same day I pushed away all of my emotions and made myself do things I didn't want to do. Quite a few times I felt like quitting, crying, going back to the dark room and watching TV. That was when I learned that in a difficult situation, there is no one but yourself who can decide the best way to handle things. It made me a stronger person and taught me how to deal with tough situations.

As time passed, the job situation in Houston worsened. Every week for over two months, an average of 1,000 people lost their jobs. Sophia's and my efforts to find employment were going nowhere. We were still okay financially, our mortgage was covered by insurance, and our unemployment checks covered all of our expenses, but the future didn't look bright.

One day while I was picking up Robby from the JCC, the Jewish lawyer whose house we had bought stopped and asked me how things were. During our conversation, he told me that one of his very close friends was the vice president of an engineering company. He offered to ask his friend if his company could employ us. A few days later, we received a phone call from Bovay Engineers asking both Sophia and me to come in for an interview. This company was doing well because most of their work was civil engineering, which was not affected by the oil crisis. Sophia and I were very happy; we knew we had been given a rare opportunity.

Upon arriving at Bovay, we were interviewed by different department managers. Shortly thereafter, we were invited to the office of the vice president. After introducing himself, he informed us that the company's policy prevented them from hiring both husband and wife. At the same time, he assured us that one of us would be hired, and it was up to us to decide and let him know who would take the job. This was a great relief for us; we had just learned that at least one of us would be employed, get a salary, and receive medical coverage for the family.

On the way home, Sophia and I made an easy decision— she would be the one to take this job because it was more suitable for her civil engineering background. Also, I was the policyholder of the mortgage unemployment insurance, and there were still three more months of coverage left, meaning we would be able to have free mortgage payments for another three months. A few days later, Sophia got her official offer—a designer's position with a salary of $10 per hour. We were very happy because in addition to getting a decent paying job, Sophia was offered a designer's position with family health benefits.

My job search, unfortunately, wasn't getting anywhere. I knew that something different had to be done and made a decision to expand my search area to include job openings outside of Houston. I began purchasing newspapers from other large metro areas, looking for employment opportunities and sending my resume all over the country. At best, I was receiving thank you letters but no job offers. About a month after Sophia started her job, I made a decision to leave Houston and search for a job in person. I had been thinking about this for a while and decided to start my job search by driving to the East Coast.

People we had met on the way to America had settled in New York, and they convinced me that I'd be able to find employment in New York City. It was pretty scary, but I had no choice. My English was still far from being good; we didn't have a lot of extra money saved, so all I could afford to take with me was $500. I had never before traveled in the USA by car, therefore everything, from using maps to finding and staying in hotels, was new to me. However, that was nothing in comparison to the feelings I experienced with the idea of leaving Sophia and Robby in Houston. I knew it would be impossible for me to face them when I had to leave, so I made a decision to leave without telling them. I had been talking to the Tennessee Valley Authority in Knoxville, Tennessee, regarding a possible position, and the morning after I received approval from their personnel department to stop in for an interview, I left while both Sophia and Robby were still asleep.

I hung my suit and shirts, packed the rest in a suitcase, and left the house without saying goodbye around four o'clock in the morning. As I was driving away from the house, my eyes were full of tears. I was crying, and all I wanted to do was turn around. I didn't know how Sophia and Robby would react when they saw my note, I didn't know exactly where to go or where to stop, so going back home was a tempting solution. As I pulled away, I made myself concentrate on the road. I was thinking about our future after I found a job and of the moment when I would be together again with my family.

Chapter 18

About ten hours of driving and not sleeping the night before finally took a toll on me. As I was passing New Orleans, I decided to stop and rest. At the hotel, using the Yellow Pages, I identified five engineering companies and called them in the morning, asking to be interviewed. Of the five companies I called, a company that performed maintenance for refineries asked me to come in for an interview. They offered me a job right after the interview, but I had to decline. They offered me a salary of $9.50 per hour, and even though it was very tempting to accept the offer, I knew that this salary would not be enough to bring my family here. Even though I didn't land a job, the fact that I had received an offer on my first day was very encouraging.

I decided not to spend any more money on hotel rooms, and after driving for about five hours, when it started to get dark, I stopped at a rest area and fell asleep in the car. In the morning I didn't feel rested, but the fact that I had saved $40 made me feel better. After driving for another day, I stopped at a hotel in Knoxville, and in the morning I went to meet with the people at TVA. I was following the driving directions they had given me when I suddenly found myself driving on country roads in the middle of nowhere. I was afraid that I was lost but decided to continue, and after driving for about thirty minutes I saw a big plant in front of me. When I drove close to the entrance, I realized that it was a nuclear power plant. I had no idea that I'd be interviewed at a nuclear plant.

Having come from Russia, the concept that I would even be allowed to go near a nuclear facility was pretty amazing for me. At the plant two department managers interviewed me, and both of them told me that they could use my engineering knowledge. I was very happy and couldn't believe that I might be working at a nuclear plant. In the waiting room I was already making plans for moving Sophia and Robby here and thought that, most likely, we would rent an apartment in the big city, and I would have to drive to work. But when I was called to the personnel department, I was told that unfortunately, I was not eligible for that position due to the fact that I was not a US citizen, and this was a working nuclear facility. That was a huge disappointment for me. Moments before, I had expected to be working in the prestigious nuclear industry, making $15 per hour and reuniting with my family, but in the blink of an eye, I was back to having none of that. All I could do for the rest of the day was to drive back to the hotel, get a small bottle of vodka, a Big Mac from McDonald's, and get drunk.

The next morning I was on the road again, and after reaching the DC area, I managed to get another interview as well as an offer for a draftsman's position. Again, as I had done in New Orleans, I declined the offer because of the low pay. The next day I finally was on my way to New York. I was very scared to drive in New York City, so I made arrangements with my friend, who used to live in Houston but moved to New York after his divorce, to meet me as soon as I entered Manhattan from the Manhattan Bridge. We agreed to meet a few blocks away from the bridge. As I approached the bridge, I suddenly realized that there was a problem; this bridge had two levels, and I didn't know which one to take. Without knowing what to do, I took the upper level, and of course when I made it to the street, my friend wasn't there to meet me. As I slowed down looking for him, I received a lot of not-so-welcome signs from New York drivers. They were not very happy with me driving slowly; they gave me very angry looks, showed their middle fingers, and blew their horns. It was very intimidating. It wasn't anything like driving in Texas. After I circled around and made a few turns, I ended up on the other side of the bridge again and this time used the lower level. A few blocks from the bridge I spotted my friend, who was patiently waiting for me. He took over the driving, and we were on the way to Brooklyn, where he was sharing an apartment with his parents.

After being under tremendous pressure during the whole week, it felt good to relax and let someone else drive. The lights of Manhattan were magnificent, and for a brief moment I even forgot about the realities of life while enjoying the scenery. Reality, however, quickly returned as we parked my car and walked to my friend's apartment. Almost everyone around us spoke Russian, and at the small store where we stopped to buy bread, the clerk's unfriendliness made me feel like I was back in Russia. The two-bedroom apartment was small, and I had to sleep on a couch in the living room. In addition, the apartment didn't have an air conditioner, and the temperature was so hot that I couldn't sleep.

In the morning, after checking the Yellow Pages, I realized that Brooklyn didn't have a lot of companies where I could apply for a job. I chose five companies, and by the end of the day I had dropped off my resume with all of them. It was a very hot day, and because I didn't want to drive, I walked all day long. When I made it back, I sat in my car, turned on the air conditioner and enjoyed the moment. I also decided to sleep in the car. I knew that another sleepless night would destroy me, and I wouldn't be able to continue my job search. It wasn't very comfortable, and every few hours I had to turn the engine on to cool off the car, but I managed to sleep most of the night. In the morning I went to the apartment, took a shower, put on my suit, picked up my briefcase with my resumes, and was on my way to Manhattan.

The New York metro shocked me. It was dirty, and the smell was terrible. Stepping out from the metro in Manhattan shocked me even more. Being surrounded by high-rise buildings made me feel very uncomfortable, and the trash all over the streets didn't help. When I entered the lobby of the first high-rise building, I saw a directory listing the companies in the building. After selecting what I believed were engineering companies, I tried to get an interview with them. Only a few times did I have the opportunity to speak to someone other than a receptionist but received no interview offers.

For ten days I walked the streets of Manhattan, entering every office building, trying to get an interview. Every day it got harder for me to do it. I was losing hope and didn't know what to do next. Coming back to Brooklyn in the evening was even harder; my friend and his parents told me that after ten days of trying I should either look for a non-engineering job or go back to Texas. That wasn't helpful, and I was trying to spend as little time as possible in their apartment.

Our friends whom we met on the way to America invited me to stay with them for a few days, and for the first time in two weeks I ended up sleeping in a normal bed, in an air-conditioned apartment. While staying with them, they gave me the idea to look for a job outside of New York City. I liked that, and during the next four days I traveled to New Jersey. I had a lot of interviews at different plants but no job offers. By the end of my third week in New York, almost all of my money was gone, and I began to think that it was time for me to look for a job as a store clerk or become a taxi driver in order to make some money. It was extremely hard even to think that I would end up doing something like that, but I had no choice; I had to survive.

While I was in New York, Sophia and I developed a system for us to communicate. She knew the times I'd be at my friend's apartment and would call during those times. To save money, I hardly called her, but the evening I decided to start the search for a non-engineering job, I called home from a pay phone. Sophia didn't try to talk me out of it; we agreed that I should do this as a temporary step. I also talked to Robby during this call. He cried and asked me to come home.

After hanging up, I felt terrible and spent the evening in my car thinking about my next steps. There were no people in New York I could talk to about my situation. That evening was one of the lowest points of my life in America. I didn't know what to do and didn't have anywhere to go. I walked to a bar and got drunk. It was around two a.m. when they told me that the bar was closed. I walked back to my car and fell asleep there. I felt terrible in the morning, and I went to my friend's apartment to shower and have a cup of coffee. When I showed up there, nobody even asked me where I had spent the last few days. They were ready for me to leave.

I asked my friend to show me what a taxi driver's day looked like. He agreed, and I had a firsthand experience of New York driving and the rudeness of the New York passengers. At the end of the day I knew that if I had to work as a taxi driver, it was going to be on a temporary basis only and that at any cost, I would be back doing what I liked to do best—working as an engineer. We made it back to his apartment around six p.m.; it was dinnertime, and since I wasn't welcome there, I decided to go for a walk. I didn't feel good and was very hungry. There was a Russian store near their apartment, and I decided to buy some bread and cheese and eat in my car. Later I went to my friend's apartment to take a shower.

As I prepared to leave my friend's apartment, the phone rang—it was Sophia asking to talk to me. It wasn't our usual call time; I knew that something important had happened for her to call. Sophia told me that there was a message on our answering machine. Bechtel, the company everyone was dreaming to work for, had left a message asking me to come for an interview on Saturday morning at nine a.m. They were looking for engineers for a nuclear power plant being constructed in Midland, Michigan and were holding an open house at the Adams Mark hotel in Houston. My first reaction was that I had a very small chance of getting a position at the nuclear construction site, but I also remembered that I'd made a decision to get an engineering job at any price, so I told Sophia that I would be there Friday. I was very excited, and the biggest reason for my excitement was the fact that I'd be back home, together with Sophia and Robby. My friend and his parents had different reasons to be happy when I told them that I would be leaving for Houston early the next morning.

I left New York around five o'clock on Thursday morning, knowing that I would have to make it to Houston by Friday evening. There were 1,800 miles in front of me—it wouldn't be an easy trip. Every eight or ten hours of driving, I stopped at a rest area, took a quick one-hour nap, and then continued my drive. I had no choice but to be in Houston by Friday night. Before noon on Friday, as I passed New Orleans, for the first time I actually began to believe that I'd make it to Houston on time. After passing Baton Rouge, I stopped to buy some food and take a nap. After napping for an hour I began the final leg of my drive to Houston. Suddenly I felt that the air from the A/C vents wasn't cool anymore; my A/C had stopped working. It was the middle of July, the outside temperature was around 100, and the humidity was also approaching 100%. I drove with my windows down until another problem arose. It began raining, and I had to roll up the windows. It became so hot inside the car that I had to stop until the rain let up.

It felt great when I could finally see the lights of Houston in front of me, and just after ten p.m. I finally made it home. Sophia and Robby were waiting; Robby would not let me out of his sight, and he even went with me to the bathroom when I took a shower. After the shower, all I could do was ask Sophia to get my suit ready, set my alarm, and without even having a bite to eat, I fell asleep. Around six a.m. I woke up, had some coffee, and was on my way to the hotel. I knew that this was going to be one of the most important days of my life; I *had* to get this job. I was afraid that if Sophia and Robby were awake, I might get emotional, so I left while they were still asleep.

I arrived at the hotel two hours prior to my appointment. Waiting in the car, I tried to develop a strategy of how to convince Bechtel's interviewers to hire me. As I walked to the lobby, I made myself believe that nothing would stop me today from getting this job. In the lobby a lot of Bechtel employees greeted me along with over fifty other applicants. After completing the paperwork, I was asked to wait in the lobby before being invited in for the interview.

Finally I was shown to a room where four Bechtel employees were studying my application together with my resume. I was extremely nervous, feeling much the same as I felt when entering the office of the Russian KGB general. After introducing myself, I immediately told the people in the room that they would never regret hiring me. I don't know why I did it, but it got their attention. They all stopped reading, looked at me, and with a smile on his face, one of them asked me to explain why would I say that. Later, when I was working for Bechtel, my immediate supervisor, who was one of my interviewers, told me that my bold statement actually was one of the reasons I got the job—they could see how determined I was. For the next thirty minutes I answered questions about my experience as well as my background.

Their biggest concern was the nonexistence of any nuclear experience in my background. I tried very hard to reassure my interviewers that I would quickly learn the new field and in no time would reach a level similar to an experienced nuclear construction engineer, similar to what happened at my first job in America. I told them about my experience in Tennessee and that the only reason I hadn't been hired for a job in the nuclear industry was because I wasn't a citizen. I said that I knew citizenship was not a problem in a nonworking plant. I also told them how I had found my first job without knowing the most important thing—the English language. We ended up talking about my drive from New York, and at the end I told them that I couldn't afford not to be hired that day.

I was asked to wait in the lobby because one of my interviewers wanted me to talk to his boss, who was the pipe support lead engineer. His name was Paul Siebert, and after he told me the job descriptions for the positions he needed to fill, I immediately replied that I could do it. I also told him that with my experience in the petrochemical industry and my willingness to work, I would be one of his best engineers and I would achieve it quickly. I pretty much guaranteed that I'd be the hardest working person he had ever seen. He told me that he was very impressed with my achievements and that I would probably get the job. He told me to expect a letter within a few weeks.

I couldn't accept this; I couldn't take the risk that someone else might get the job, and I asked Paul if he could make an exception, review my resume, consider my situation, and make me an offer that day. I could see the confusion on his face. He tried to explain that they didn't have all the necessary personnel in Houston to make the final decisions.

Only after I told him that during the last five months I'd heard the same answer many times and that after leaving the interview today I wouldn't expect to hear from him, Paul told me to wait in the room, and he left. I didn't know what to expect, and as I was thinking about what to do next, Paul and another man entered the room. The man with him was the manager of all engineering. I was expecting more questions about my previous work and more technical questions in general. Instead, he asked me to tell him how I got my first job in Houston. I didn't expect a nonworking-related question, and it took me a few moments to understand what he wanted to know. I told them the story of the drawing I had made to use for my interviews and how the drawing helped me get my first job. The engineering manager told me that this story was in line with what Paul had told him about me. He also told me with a smile that he was glad to meet me—the person who refused to leave the building without an offer.

My answer was that without an offer, I had no choice but to go back to New York and work as a taxi driver to feed my family. I also told him that engineering was my passion and asked him to hire me. After asking me to wait in the room again, both of them stepped out. I knew that during the next few minutes my life could be changed forever.

Again, as it happened when I was waiting for the Russian general to make his decision, I got the feeling that I would be okay no matter what decision was made. Somehow I got this feeling that regardless of what may happen in the next few minutes, I would end up working for Bechtel. When the door opened, Paul informed me that the engineering manager had decided to make an exception and was ready to make me an offer today. I almost fainted and had to hold onto the chair. Paul brought some papers with him, asking me to read the terms of my employment and saying that if the terms were acceptable to me, I would be hired today. I honestly didn't care about the terms; all I wanted to know was the salary they were offering.

After learning that they would be paying me $13 an hour, I immediately signed the papers, and that was the beginning of my new engineering chapter working in the nuclear industry. After signing a few more papers, Paul and the engineering manager told me that the package with the official offer, details, and instructions would be mailed to me in a few days.

I was so excited about being hired that I had to sit and cool down for almost an hour before feeling comfortable enough to drive home. As I drove home I realized what just happened to me and how drastically my life had changed during the last hour. It felt great because I hadn't given up; I had made it through the hardest times in my life, and most importantly, I did it all by myself.

Chapter 19

While driving home from my successful interview, I thought of my dad, knowing how proud of my achievements he would be. It was so unfair that he wasn't alive anymore; I wanted so badly to talk to him. I wanted to share what had just happened to me, and my eyes were brimming with tears. At home I was met as a hero after breaking the news about getting a job in the nuclear industry. We celebrated my job offer and made a decision that Sophia and Robby would stay in Houston while I would work in Midland. I also decided that my job search for a position in the Houston area would not end with this offer. The decision to move and live alone, away from Sophia and Robby, was not an easy one. I knew Robby would be very upset with this decision, so we didn't tell him until the last few days. We also determined that Sophia and Robby would be better off if they moved from the house into an apartment. The next day we put up a For Sale sign in front of our house, and the same day one of our neighbors came over asking us questions about the house because his cousin was looking to buy a house in the neighborhood. I told my neighbor that his cousin could move in without any down payment. All we needed was for him to take over our monthly payments.

Within a few days we signed the papers and officially sold our house. It was unbelievable to sell a house in Houston without losing any money because every day hundreds of homeowners were simply moving out of their houses, unable to make mortgage payments and ruining their credit history. By the end of the week I received the package with the official offer from Bechtel. They offered to move my family, my household goods, and pay a week of my salary to cover my traveling cost in addition to covering a month of my stay at a Midland hotel. Even though all of that was almost too good to be true, I really couldn't fully enjoy it because of my fast-approaching departure date.

While Sophia was at work, Robby and I spent a lot of time together. Almost every morning we went to the Jewish Community Center, the zoo, or for walks in the parks. Finally, I decided to tell Robby that in a few days I would be leaving for Michigan because I had found a job there. This made him very upset, and for the rest of the day he kept asking me how long I would be there. I didn't have an answer, and I didn't want to lie. I remember telling Robby that I would start looking for a job in Houston from the day I started working in Michigan. I also asked Robby to help me with my job search in Houston by checking the employment section of the *Houston Chronicle* and let me know of any new engineering job offers. Robby became very happy and excited over being involved in my job search. We also made a promise to talk to each other on a daily basis.

As my departure day approached, I had mixed feelings. I was very upset because I would have to leave alone, but I was happy about getting paychecks again and learning a brand new industry. Actually, there was another reason I wanted to leave. A lot of our Russian friends had become very jealous about my success and couldn't hide it. When we would meet at the Jewish Community Center during my last few weeks, some were accusing me of lying about my new job. Some were convinced that the real reason I was leaving Houston was to become a taxi driver in New York. I was also accused of lying about our house sale because in their minds nobody could do it, so they assumed that I, like everyone else, had walked away from our house. All of that was very upsetting to me. I never expected to hear that from some of the people I had considered friends just a few months ago.

I was planning to leave Houston as soon as I moved Sophia and Robby to the new apartment, which we were planning to do within three days. However, a bad hurricane was expected to hit Houston the next day. Hurricane Alicia was a very strong Category 3 storm, and it was very scary when it hit. Sophia and Robby felt comfortable with me being home and monitoring the situation; they even fell asleep. It felt great to see them relaxed and asleep during such a bad storm. It was about two o'clock in the morning when the winds peaked at about 80 miles per hour, and the house was shaking slightly. It was very scary; I panicked and woke up Sophia and Robby. The safest place was the closet, and all of us hid in there for a few hours. Fortunately, our house wasn't seriously damaged; only a small piece of the outside wall came loose. The damage was minor, and I was able to fix it myself after the storm passed.

The apartment complex where Sophia and Robby were moving wasn't damaged, and within a few days we moved in. At the same time, the moving company picked up the furniture I decided to take with me to Midland: a couch, a kitchen table, and four chairs. Finally, it was time for me to leave. According to my employment contract I was allowed five traveling days with pay.

I remember well the evening before leaving Houston. I was very sad, but this time it felt nothing like the time I had to go to New York. This time I knew that I was going to be making money, enabling me to support my family. I was also looking forward to seeing Mark, who was already working in Midland. He had transferred from Houston a few months before I was hired. This time I was going to a new place knowing that I had a very good friend there and that I wouldn't be alone. As I had done when leaving for New York, I left the apartment before Sophia and Robby woke up, and again, tears filled my eyes as I drove away from Houston. I decided to shorten my trip to just two days. I didn't want to be alone, and I felt that being with Mark would make it much easier on me. The first day, I drove more than half of the distance before stopping at a hotel, and I was on the road again very early the next morning.

I was so determined to be in Midland before dark that I almost killed myself. About 100 miles from Midland, I fell asleep behind the wheel. It was a terrifying incident; when I opened my eyes, the car was driving off the road on the opposite side. I was very lucky that there were no other cars close by, and I had the chance to slow down while pulling back onto the right side of the highway. My heart was beating so hard that I had to stop. It took at least ten minutes before I felt comfortable enough to drive again. At the first rest area I called Sophia, telling her about what just happened, talking for almost thirty minutes.

After the call and an hour's nap I was on the road again, arriving at Midland well after dark. Shortly after checking in at a Holiday Inn, Mark showed up, and seeing him made me feel good and relaxed. I knew that I had a very good friend, someone I could count on, someone who would help me get through a tough time in my life. Today our friendship is stronger than ever. We feel like brothers and talk daily. I don't know where I would be today without Mark's friendship and help when I needed it most.

A few days later I began my new job. I was assigned to the Field Mechanical Engineering group, solving field issues related to piping and pipe supports. During the first week all I did was read procedures, get safety training, and feel pretty good about my job. All of that changed when, at the beginning of my second week, a fellow engineer took me on a tour of the reactor building, where I would be spending most of my time. What a shocking experience that was. In my wildest dreams, I couldn't imagine the existence of what I saw—I was surrounded by thousands of pipes, pipe supports, and very large equipment. Some of the pumps were twenty feet tall, and some pipe supports were much taller than I. The round dome was at least 120 feet above ground level, and there were five levels below the ground.

It took at least a week of me walking around inside the building, getting lost quite a few times, and finding the exit after being lost before I finally started to feel more comfortable being there. It took me a few more weeks until I began to feel comfortable with the terminology and, most importantly, began understanding the craftsmen I was assigned to work with. I also realized that there were a lot of similarities between the petrochemical and nuclear industries, so by using my engineering knowledge and common sense I was making a lot of good problem-solving decisions. The craftsmen I was assigned to work with recognized my work and felt very comfortable implementing the changes I made for them. Paul, the person who interviewed me in Houston, ended up being my supervisor on the site and was also very pleased with my work. I remember a few months into my employment he told me that he was very happy with my performance and had no regrets regarding their decision to hire me on the spot.

Everything was going well in my professional life, but my personal life was a different story. The long distance started to take a toll on our relationship. I tried very hard to make sure I was a part of Robby's life and talked to him every day. It was hard—he was always asking me when I would come home, and I had no answers. All I could do was tell him that I was looking for a job in Houston every day and that I always followed the leads he gave me each Sunday.

After spending a month in the hotel, I moved to a one-bedroom apartment across the parking lot from Mark. He was sharing a two-bedroom apartment with a co-worker from Houston. Mark and I spent all of our free time together. We would drive to different places in Michigan and even crossed the Canadian border a few times. Mark was very good at recognizing edible mushrooms, and quite often we would to go to the forest and, within a few hours, we'd pick a full bucket of mushrooms, cook them, and have food for a few days. We also pickled the mushrooms and stored them in the refrigerator. This was one of the best forms of relaxation for me, but it ended when the first snow covered the ground.

The first week of December, I flew back to Houston to visit Sophia and Robby. I spent two days in Houston, and it was great to be together. Unfortunately, I also got the feeling that our family would be in jeopardy if our separation continued. I decided it was time to get serious about finding a job back in the Houston area. Unfortunately, the petrochemical industry still hadn't recovered, but I learned that Ebasco, an engineering company based in New York, was designing and constructing a nuclear power plant about 105 miles southwest of Houston, near Bay City. After contacting Ebasco and finding the name of the person in the personnel department overseeing this project, I wrote a letter to him explaining the reasons for my need to move back to Houston, and I mailed it together with my resume to him. In a few weeks, I received a standard letter from

Ebasco saying that they were impressed with my resume and would keep it on file. I knew that it meant absolutely nothing, so I decided to call their New York office on a bi-weekly basis. I knew that my only chance of being hired was to keep my name at the forefront for the time when they would be looking for more employees.

When I called, I always asked for the same person, asked the same question, and after a few weeks we became friendly, even discussing personal issues. I had a good feeling about being on his priority list to be called, should they start hiring. Somewhere toward the end of December he told me that there might be a possibility that new positions would need to be filled by Ebasco sometime in April or May, and that was very encouraging.

Unfortunately, I couldn't go home to celebrate New Year's 1984 with my family. Mark went home, and I had to spend New Year's Eve all by myself, sitting in my empty apartment, drinking cognac. It was the first time in my life that I was alone on New Year's Eve, and it felt terrible. I remember well my New Year's resolution: to be back in Houston within six months, with or without a job.

Sophia accumulated some vacation days at her job, and in February she and Robby came to visit me in Midland. They spent three days with me, and that was the best time I'd had in a long time. It was very hard to say goodbye; Robby cried so hard at the airport that I had to run out of the terminal because I didn't want him to see me crying.

The very next morning I called my Ebasco contact to discuss my personal problems and ask for his help. After talking to me for a while, he promised to arrange an interview for me. He even told me to expect a phone call within a week. During the next few days I was afraid to leave my desk. In order to get my work done, I came to work very early, finished the fieldwork before ten a.m., and worked at my desk even during my lunch break. Finally, by the end of the week I received the phone call. I couldn't believe it when I was told that my interview with Ebasco had been arranged. I was told to show up at the Bay City location in two weeks. I felt like jumping up and down but kept my emotions under control while talking. I wasn't even listening to what he was saying. I answered yes and agreed to everything he asked.

Chapter 20

The next two weeks were probably among the slowest weeks in my life. I couldn't wait to fly back to Houston. At the airport I rented a car, drove home, and spent the evening with Sophia and Robby. In the morning I left for Bay City, about 105 miles away. I was very scared because I didn't have enough experience for Ebasco's open positions, but I also knew that this was my only chance to move back to Houston quickly. It took me almost two hours to get to the plant, and by the time I arrived, I was prepared to do the same as I had done a few months ago to get this job no matter what. After a short interview with the personnel department manager, I was told that Manny G., the assistant principal engineer for the entire project, would talk to me shortly.

We had a very long meeting. Manny asked me a lot of engineering questions, and to my relief, the majority of his questions were about engineering in general, not related to the nuclear industry. Somehow, both of us felt comfortable also talking about our personal lives. He told me about his family's journey from Cuba to the USA, and I told him about ours. I also told him that I was running a great risk of losing my wife and son, should I not move back very soon. I even asked if it would be possible to get an offer today. Unfortunately, it didn't work this time. When saying goodbye, he told me that he liked both the professional and personal parts of our interview and would make his recommendation to his superiors soon. As I left the plant, I had mixed feelings. I was disappointed that I hadn't received an offer on the spot, but I had a very good feeling about Manny and my interview with him. I knew that if the decision to hire was made strictly on my professional experience I probably would not qualify, but something kept my hopes up. Somehow I knew that Manny would be looking at more than my professional and especially nuclear experience.

After spending the weekend in Houston, I was back in Midland, and again, as it had been while waiting for a call to set the interview, time seemed to stand still during the next two weeks. At the beginning of the third week I couldn't help it and called New York for an update. My contact at the personnel department explained that this was a normal process, that the people from Texas should send the details to him, and then he would prepare the offer. A few more weeks passed without any news, and I was losing hope of moving back to Houston. I really didn't have any way to influence Ebasco's decision; however, I decided that I'd go back to Houston within a few months even without their offer. I had Manny's phone number and was hoping to get in touch with him when I got back to Houston.

I had almost lost my hopes of getting the job when one day, just before lunchtime, the phone on my desk rang. It was my contact from New York telling me that he was ready to make me an offer. When I realized that this was for real, I almost fainted. He asked me if it would be better for us to talk in the evening, when I was at home. I don't know what gave me the strength to tell him that calling in the evening would be much better for me. Immediately after we hung up I panicked about my decision not to talk to him. I became afraid he might not call me back in the evening. I had to share this with Mark, and together we went to the reactor building, pretending we were working. Mark tried to reassure me that I had done the right thing; he was sure that my move would make their offer even better. Talking to Mark helped me cool down, and soon we found ourselves discussing what would I have to do to get him a job over there. Mark was also trying very hard to find a job in the Houston area because he wanted to be close to his parents and brother. I couldn't wait for the day to be over, and after work both Mark and I went to my apartment.

Shortly after the phone rang, and it was the man from the personnel department telling me that Ebasco was happy to make me an offer for a field pipe support engineering position at the south Texas nuclear station. I wanted to scream yes without even hearing the facts and conditions, but I kept calm and let him continue. He told me that my starting salary would be $15 per hour with time and a half for overtime. I was very happy with the salary and the position and was ready to say yes to the offer. However, before I accepted the offer he continued, telling me that because I was coming from another state, Ebasco would pay me per diem. It was a $50 tax-free allowance per day, including weekends and holidays. He also told me that they would cover my moving expenses. All of that sounded unreal to me; I didn't expect any extras and immediately accepted their offer, with a starting day in three weeks.

I'll never forget the phone call to Sophia and Robby. What a great feeling it was when telling them about my offer and that I'd be back in Houston in less than three weeks. Against all odds I had won—not only was I moving back, I was coming back on a "white horse." I would be working for a very good company and getting a great salary with per diem pay. Two weeks and one day after receiving the job offer, I was on my way to Houston.

Back in Houston, we decided that it would be the best if I commuted to Bay City. Sophia had a very good job she didn't want to quit, and Robby was very happy at his school. I was content with any arrangement. It didn't even bother me that the distance between our apartment and the job site was about 105 miles and that in order to be at the job site by six a.m., I would have to leave the apartment at four a.m. To my surprise I found quite a few people who were commuting from Houston, and I had no problem joining a carpool with three other engineers. I had to drive only twice a week and was able to nap when not driving. On a normal day I would usually come home after seven p.m. and was very tired. However, I didn't want Robby to see how tired I was, and quite often after a quick dinner we would do something together, like play basketball or go to the JCC for a swim.

Things were going well for me at work. I was working very hard applying the knowledge I had gained during my employment in Michigan, and my immediate supervisor was very happy with my work. There were at least three layers of supervision between Manny and me, but he made me feel very comfortable about discussing work-related issues and solutions to field problems directly with me. Quite often after discussing a work-related question, we would end up talking about our families and other nonwork-related issues. I knew that without his help I wouldn't have been working there, and I made sure he knew how appreciative I was. I also had to make sure he would never regret hiring me—the promise I had made during my interview. Manny wanted to meet my family, so he invited us to his house. Our families became friends, and even now, decades later, we stay in touch regularly by talking over the phone and attending each other's family celebrations.

At the end of the third month, I was asked to go to Manny's office. I was surprised to see the piping manager there and even more surprised when he asked me to accept a promotion and to become the group leader of the pipe support team. It meant that I would be in charge and responsible for twenty field engineers. I didn't know if I was ready for a such challenging job; not only would I have to supervise more experienced American engineers, but I'd also have to participate in the daily morning coordination meetings with other disciplines. Manny, who was in charge of all engineering, assured he would help me if should I need it. He also told me that with the promotion my salary would increase to $17 per hour. I was scared but accepted the promotion on the spot and never had any regrets about that decision.

Shortly after being promoted I told Manny about Mark. I had told Manny about Mark's engineering knowledge and that having him work in my group would help me achieve our goals much easier. Manny agreed to interview Mark, and within a few weeks Mark arrived for an interview. After a short interview with Manny, both of them walked to my office, and with a smile on his face, Manny told me that it would be up to me whether to hire Mark, then he left us alone. It didn't take long for Mark to get the offer, and both of us were very happy. Mark was returning to Houston to be close to his family, and I was getting back the friend I could count on. In less than a month Mark began working in my group. He also decided to commute from Houston, so we began to carpool together. Since it was only the two of us carpooling, it gave me the opportunity to work longer hours and allowed Mark to work overtime, approved by me.

I quickly became very good at scheduling, coordinating, and solving problems, and most importantly I was gaining more self-confidence. So many times when nobody knew how to solve a problem, Mark and I would go to the field together and solve it. Both of us had an advantage over American engineers who were trained and had great knowledge in one discipline—Russia's colleges had taught us a wider range of knowledge in many disciplines. This wide base of knowledge helped me to better understand and better coordinate work efforts with other departments. Since the coordination between the piping, HVAC, and electrical departments was the key to success for the pipe support group, I became very a valuable employee.

To solve many field problems, I went to different buildings a few times daily. There was no air conditioning in the buildings, so the temperature inside some of the small rooms where we worked reached well over 100° Fahrenheit. Pretty soon I learned to bring a spare pair of jeans and extra shirts to work, and quite often I had to change my clothes after such field trips. I was working a lot of overtime and we were saving a lot of money, which once again brought us a sense of financial security. It didn't help my personal life, however.

Long work hours and a lot of responsibilities began to put a dent in our relationship. When at home between seven in the evening and four in the morning, the best I could do was to spend an hour with Robby and Sophia, grab some food and go to bed. I wanted to do more for both my son and my wife, but I also knew that my job was the way to secure my family's future, so I tried very hard to find the perfect balance. As my work had been entering some critical stages, I had to spend even more hours there. Because we worked very late most days, Mark and I decided to rent an apartment in Bay City. I came to Houston a few times a week and usually spent Sundays with my family. It was a very difficult lifestyle for all of us, and the only bright point in all that was my paycheck.

Shortly after my one-year anniversary with Ebasco, Manny asked me to accept a new position. My main responsibilities would be coordinating work between piping, mechanical, pipe supports, and HVAC disciplines. It also meant that I would have over fifty field engineers reporting to me. He told me that he was very comfortable offering this position to me, and I agreed to take on the additional responsibilities. It actually made my life a little easier because I learned how to delegate more responsibilities to each group leader, giving me a chance to spend more time with my family. Immediately after accepting the new position, I asked Manny to promote Mark to the position I had vacated, and without any hesitation, he agreed. It was a great relief because I then knew that my involvement in the pipe support group would be minimal, and I also could count on Mark keeping me informed of any problems with other group leaders.

In Houston I was asked by a friend to help a Russian immigrant find employment. Yakov had been without a job for a long period of time. He had a degree in aviation mechanics from St. Petersburg University. I remember our first meeting well —we invited both his wife and him to our apartment. He didn't look very healthy: he was pale and very thin. We spoke for a while, and it didn't take long for me to understand that this man would do the job well and would be a good asset to the team. I explained the working conditions at STP, and he answered that he would do any kind of work. I also remember that after they left our apartment, Sophia made me promise to do everything in my power to get him hired.

After telling Manny about my meeting with Yakov, an interview was scheduled. Manny told me that by now, when he saw a hard-to-pronounce last name, especially if it was a Russian engineer, he was willing to give the person a try. After the interview, Manny told me that his head was telling him "no way" about hiring Yakov—he had no experience, and his English was poor; however, his heart was telling him to hire him. A few days later Yakov was hired as a field pipe support engineer, and Mark quickly trained him to become a very good field engineer.

Because of my ability to better delegate responsibilities, I was able to go home almost every day, and my personal life began to improve. We also moved from the small apartment to a nice condominium across the street from the Jewish Community Center.

I spoke to my mom and Polina on regular basis. Polina told me that she had met a nice man, and they were planning to get married soon. She assured me that they'd be in America as soon as they could get permission to leave. Shortly after their wedding they applied to get permission. Unfortunately, for the third time the KGB denied them permission to leave. I decided to get proactive here in the USA. One of my co-workers introduced me to then-Senator Lloyd Bentsen. At his residence in Port Lavaca, I asked if he could help me reunite with my mom and my sister's family. Unfortunately, I later received a phone call from the senator informing me that there were no more avenues for him to try. He also scared me by telling me that the Russians knew about my work in the nuclear industry and would rather see me back in Russia than allow my mom and sister to leave. All of that happened during our application process to become US citizens. During this process we were allowed to change our last name, and we decided to use this opportunity, thinking it would be harder for the Russians to track us down. By using first letters from our last and first names (N, A, S) our new last name was born.

During the same time, we suddenly got an unexpected financial break. Our landlord declared bankruptcy and wouldn't cash our rent checks. We lived rent-free for six months, and that helped us to build up a significant amount of savings.

Sophia was doing extremely well at her job, and when the company she was working for purchased the CAD system, Sophia was asked to be in charge and was sent for a week of training to Kansas City. That was a huge promotion for her.

Everything was going well for us, and we decided it was time for us to have a second child. We always wanted to have more kids. A few months later we learned that Sophia was pregnant. At the time both of us were heavy smokers, however as soon as Sophia learned that she was pregnant, she quit smoking. I stopped smoking at home, and after gradually reducing my nicotine intake at work only, I also quit. Prior to that I had tried unsuccessfully to quit smoking. This time I knew that I had no choice but to quit and did it by slowly reducing my daily allowance. It was working well until I was on my last step, the one-cigarette-per-day allowance. I couldn't wait to be in my office early in the morning, get my cup of coffee, and enjoy a cigarette. It took me almost three months to finally give up this pleasure. Sophia and I haven't touched another cigarette since 1987.

Chapter 21

Mom and Polina arrived in America
Michael my brother in law, Mom, me
Sara, Michael's Mom, Polina, Sam, Michael's Dad, Robby
Suzie, Michael, Sophia

After being in the country for five years, we were allowed to apply for US citizenship, and within one year we became citizens of the United States of America. We took the oath on December 20, 1986. For us, it was a very significant moment in our lives. After being country-less for more than six years, we became citizens of the greatest country in the world. Quite a few times I have tried to describe our feelings on that day and came to the conclusion that it's an impossible task. All I can say is that it was a great day in our lives. Almost immediately after becoming US citizens, we invited Sophia's parents in Israel to move to the USA. They were happy to move and to be close to both their children and grandchildren.

Everything was going well at my work, we were getting closer to finishing Unit #1, and the completion of Unit #2 would take another three years to complete. I knew that I would be transferred to another project upon completion and felt very secure at work. At the same time that we were getting ready to work on Unit #2, Ebasco teamed up with Bechtel for a feasibility study at the unfinished nuclear station in Glen Rose, Texas. The work at Comanche Peak Nuclear Power Plant was on hold because the general contractor, Brown & Root, had some serious problems with the Nuclear Regulatory Commission. The project also had two units, and both of them were partially completed. To do the feasibility study for Comanche Peak station, Ebasco assembled a team of eighteen engineers to be sent there and to perform a complete walk-down and assessment of the existing installed systems. I was one of the eighteen engineers. We were told that it was a six-month temporary assignment, and because it was only a four-hour drive from Houston, Sophia and I decided that it would be best if I initially went by myself.

By that time Sophia was already six months pregnant, and I agreed to it only because Sophia's parents had already arrived from Israel and moved in with us. As soon as I left, both Sophia and I realized that not being together was not a good idea. Ebasco was paying for all my living expenses, including per diem, and we decided that by the end of May, when Robby's school ended, all of them would temporarily move to Fort Worth. Again, it was Mark who helped us; he drove Sophia to Fort Worth to go house hunting and helped her back in Houston when it was time to pack.

By the beginning of May, we learned that Texas Utilities would go ahead with the completion of the Comanche Peak Power Plant. They decided to replace Brown & Root as the general contractor and awarded the management to Bechtel. A good friend of mine, Michael M., who was in charge of Bechtel's group at Comanche Peak, offered me a position with Bechtel. They offered more money, better per diem, a management position, and a job that would last a minimum of six years. They also paid for my family's moving expenses. Manny had no objections to me taking this job, so I switched companies.

We rented a three-bedroom duplex at Altamesa Boulevard in Fort Worth and spent the next two years living there. I had it easy this time; instead of a 105-mile drive, I had to drive only fifty-five miles each way to get to my job. At the job site we were walking down the systems, checking the as-built conditions against the design drawings, and estimating the amount of time and money needed to complete the job. Most days I was home around six o'clock in the evening and didn't have to work on weekends.

At six-twenty p.m. on August 27, 1987, our son, Michael, was born at the All Saints hospital. This was a very happy day for us; we became parents again of a beautiful child and felt proud of our ability to take very good care of our family of four. Having a new son also meant something very important to me—I was able to name him after my dad. Michael's middle name, Steven, came from my grandfather's name Shlomo.

Michael's birth allowed me to experience and participate in something I couldn't even dream of when living in Russia—I was in the room with Sophia when Michael was born, actually holding her hands. And then to hold my son just moments after he was born was one of the highlights in my life.

Sophia's parents were a big help to us, not only because we didn't have to worry about cooking and cleaning—they also helped Sophia take care of Michael. Unfortunately, lack of English and the inability to drive made them move to Los Angeles, where Sam had been living for over two years. They moved to West Hollywood, where they could live independently in a very large Russian-speaking community. Even though it was hard for them to make this move, in the long-term it turned to be the right one. They became completely independent and self-sustaining in West Hollywood.

My job situation was getting even better. I was promoted to lead all HVAC work including the engineering, field engineering, and quality control departments. It felt great. I couldn't believe that I was supervising over sixty engineers, and most of them were American engineers. My salary had increased, and I was continuing to receive my tax-free daily $50 per diem.

Sophia didn't go back to work until Michael turned seven months old, at which time my co-worker's wife, Cindy Barth, who was taking care of her own two children, agreed to take care of Michael.

Meanwhile, in Russia, things were changing for the better. As the Soviet Union began to break down, my mom and Polina quickly applied again for permission to leave. Finally, in March of 1989, all of them received the long-awaited permission. The news made us very happy. It was hard to believe that after nine years of waiting, soon we would be together again.

This was also the time in our life when both Sophia and I began to realize that in order to secure our future we would need to settle down and start our own business. We were looking forward, realizing that working in the engineering fields would require us to move from one city to another in order to continue to be employed. We weren't ready to make any significant changes at that time but were exploring a few ideas, such as a partnership with our friends in a New York bagel shop or buying a bakery in Princeton. Upon visiting both places we decided that Fort Worth would be the best place for us to settle. I had a long-term good paying job, the city was the perfect size, the schools were very good, and it was a great place to raise children. Another big reason was Robby, who had made a lot of great friends there and was already attending high school.

While in Fort Worth we had been introduced to a few Russian families and had become friends with some of them. We became good friends with Isaac G. and his family, who were our age and who also had two kids.

Isaac, together with his brother-in-law Boris S., was a business owner of a few Pearle Vision stores. They moved to Fort Worth from Chicago when a business opportunity became available. When they learned about our plans to settle in Fort Worth and become business owners, Isaac offered to be on the lookout for opportunities in the optical field.

There was no urgency for us to find a business. As construction of Unit #1 was coming closer to completion, Bechtel formed a final reconciliation group, and I was asked to lead it. The purpose of this group was to walk down every system and recalculate critical issues to the as-built field conditions. Over 100 engineers, representing each discipline, were assigned to this group, and our job was to make sure that each system would work properly prior to turning it over to the client. It was a very challenging job, and I was under a lot of pressure from the client to sign off on the system, while at the same time, Bechtel was pressuring me to have zero tolerance before turning the system over. At least twice daily I attended meetings with top Bechtel and the clients' managers, updating them on the progress and explaining the reasons for each modification. It was a very fine line I had to walk, but most of the time I managed to make both sides happy.

Based on this successful operation, the client and Bechtel decided to keep this group with a scaled-down number of employees during the Unit #2 work completion. I received a very nice bonus, and it was extremely nice to hear from the top management how pleased they were with my work. Based on my success, I received a management position promotion, allowing me to receive yearly bonuses in addition to the increased salary. It wasn't just the money that made me very happy; my biggest satisfaction was that in five years, I had gone from zero to a fairly high professional level in a brand new field. For the first time since we had arrived in America, I had no more fears about my job security. I knew that after this work was completed, should we not end up owning a business, Bechtel would find a position for me at their other locations, and I would be transferred there.

During one of our dinners with Isaac's family, we were offered the opportunity to purchase a Pearle Vision store. Isaac's brother-in-law had three stores: two in Dallas and one in Fort Worth. He had decided to sell the one in Fort Worth and offered it to us. To make sure we would be doing well financially, I was planning to continue working for as long as I could. Sophia agreed to quit her job and get trained by the sellers. For three months she drove to their Dallas store every day and soon felt comfortable with all of the business aspects. We were approved by Pearle Vision Corporation, paid the asking price to the seller, and became business owners. Even though our savings were depleted, we felt comfortable. I had my job to support our lifestyle, and Sophia was confident that we would be able to make money as the business owners from day one.

December 14, 1990 was the day we purchased our first store. From day one, Sophia was in total control of our business, and as expected, we made money, even though we had two loans to repay. I was pretty amazed at how good she was in her new role, and by the end of the first year, Sophia had increased sales by 17%, receiving our first "Golden Spectacles" award from Pearle Vision.

I was also planning to learn the business, mainly going there on the weekends. At the end of the first month, however, Sophia found out that our manager, who was also our lab technician, was stealing from us. We fired him on the spot, and I had no choice but to quickly replace him as our lab technician. At the end of each day after my regular job, I drove to the store to learn and actually make the eyeglasses. I didn't have time to learn how to operate the business, but within a month I was a pretty good lab technician.

Within a year we purchased another location in Arlington, and then within another year, we purchased our third one in Denton.

As we were preparing to fully enter the business world, my mom and Polina began their journey to America. Because I was a US citizen, my mom would be arriving as an immigrant and not as a refugee. It meant that I had to take care of all her needs, including lodging, food, and medical expenses. My sister's refugee status allowed the Jewish Federation of Fort Worth to provide them with all necessary help, similar to the help provided to us in Houston.

On August 31, 1989, after nine years of separation, my mom and sister arrived in Fort Worth, and we were finally reunited. It was a very emotional reunion, and without my friend's video recording and pictures he took, I wouldn't even remember the details. The Federation rented a two-bedroom apartment for my sister, and after staying for two weeks with us at our Altamesa home, all of them, including my mom, moved there. The apartment was within walking distance of our place, so it was very convenient for us to get together almost every day. It felt so good to have my mom and sister close by. It didn't take long for us to realize that Michael, my brother-in-law, was a very good man and that my sister was in good hands. His parents also were allowed to leave Russia, and after spending a month at our place, moved to the B'nai B'rith apartments, where they spent over twenty years.

Sophia and I decided that in order for my sister and her husband to be happy and really appreciate their achievements in America, they would need to do everything, including finding a car and jobs, all by themselves. We made it very clear that we were there for any of their needs that should arise, but they would have to do everything by themselves. With our guidance, they successfully achieved everything they needed to achieve. Both of them found employment within a few months, and we were happy to see them getting comfortable in America. My mom was very happy because she was together with both her children and grandchildren, and she was also able to help us by taking care of Michael.

One day she confessed that prior to arriving in America, she hadn't been sure if I was truthful when telling her about our success. She thought that I was just trying to keep her from worrying by telling her our stories of success. She was very happy to see firsthand that everything I had told them about our achievements was real. Quite often we spoke about Dad. I missed him a lot. Mom and I talked about how this would have been a perfect time in our lives to enjoy each other. I had been too young when we left Russia and hadn't spent enough time with him. I was at the age when, in my mind, he was too old for me. I could only imagine how happy he would have been not just seeing us all together, but also seeing the quality of our lives. That was his goal—for us to be together and happy.

Unfortunately, in 1991 my mom was diagnosed with colon cancer. Surgery prolonged her life for almost two years. She passed away in June of 1993, at the age of sixty-four. We had spent only four years together in America, however I feel good about having had a chance to take her to quite a few places in the US and spend quality time together. The highlight of that was our road trip to Los Angeles. She was pretty happy to see America, and of course, to see Hollywood.

According to the Jewish law, an adult child has to recite mourner's kaddish for eleven months. Since the temple we were attending didn't have morning minyan, we switched to a conservative synagogue. I attended morning minyan for eleven months, and since I didn't do it for my dad, I decided to recite kaddish for him after finishing the required eleven months for my mom.

The morning prayers became a very important part of my life, and even after finishing the eleven months for my dad, I have never stopped going to morning minyan.

A few months after my mom's death, at age thirty-seven, when our sons were sixteen and six years old, Sophia was diagnosed with cancer. The news was terrifying and very hard to absorb. In line with the Russian way of dealing with such news, Sophia and I decided not to disclose it, and we kept it a secret from our kids in order to protect them.

Radiation treatment did its job, and since February of 1994 Sophia has been cancer free. I strongly believe that in addition to the medicine, Sophia's very strong will and lots of prayers were also key factors in her beating the cancer.

Unfortunately, radiation took a strong toll on her hearing, which got reduced to almost nothing. Again, with the help of modern medicine, a cochlear implant did its job. With it, Sophia lives a pretty normal life.

Many years later, Sophia decided to tell our kids about her medical issues. It was very hard to defend the decision to keep it a secret from them for over a decade, but eventually they understood.

After graduating Rice University, Robby attended the medical school in Galveston.

He decided to become an ear, nose, and throat physician, went to the University of Washington in Saint Louis for residency, and even spent two more years over there in the research program, trying to find ways of curing diseases that occur in many post-radiation patients like his mom.

While in Saint Louis, he met Diane, and they got married in 2009. In May of 2010 our first grandchild, Natalia, was born, and in September of 2013, we became grandparents of their second child, Max.

After moving to Austin, Robby became a partner in an ENT practice and is a very successful and well-respected surgeon.

Michael, since middle school, developed a very strong knowledge of computers. While a teenager, he built computers for our personal use at home, as well as computers for our businesses. As a matter of fact, even now, the store we just sold is still using the network Michael built.

It was no surprise that upon graduating high school, he was accepted to a very prestigious program at the University of California, Santa Barbara. Upon graduation he attended a special program to become a software engineer in San Francisco. He is very successful in his field and is working as a principal software engineer in New York.

In 1993 we got an opportunity to purchase our third store in Denton. At that time, Sophia and I decided to help my sister become a business owner. We made her and Michael, my brother-in-law, partners at this store. Polina quickly learned the business and successfully ran it until we sold it fifteen years later.

By the time we had three stores, my assignment at Comanche Peak nuclear station came to an end. To continue in the engineering business, I would have had to move to another project; at that time I was offered to move either to Tennessee or Czechoslovakia, where Bechtel was awarded the completion of a semi-finished nuclear plant. The plant was abandoned after the Soviet Union collapsed, most of the paperwork was done in the Russian language, and the offer for me to accept this assignment was incredibly attractive. After turning down all of these offers, I quit my engineering job and got more involved in the optical business.

A few years later we built a brand new store. It was our fourth one. Our strategy to sell the stores after significantly increasing sales worked very well. We eventually sold three of our stores at a profit. The only one we kept was our original store on the east side of Fort Worth, and Polina became our employee.

After purchasing the store in 1990, it took us almost seven years to change our landlord's mind and sell the land with the building to us. Even though it was a risky deal for us due to the bad reputation this part of town had, it proved to be a great move.

In 2002 after Eckerd Drugs, now CVS, built a new store across the street from us, Walgreens badly wanted to build their store on our property. After successful negotiations, we sold them half of the land. They built a brand new 2,100 square foot store for us on the second half of our land. We almost tripled the sales amounts at the store, received numerous recognitions from Pearle Vision, and were even awarded Pearle Vision's 2016 Innovator of the Year. Our deep involvement with surrounding businesses and non-profit organizations prompted the East Fort Worth Business Association to choose us for the 2016 Outstanding Business of the Year award.

In September of 2018 we sold the business, and we're now enjoying retirement.

Polina continues to work for the new owners, and Michael, her husband, has been working for the same engineering and manufacturing company for over twenty years as a project manager.

They have two children. My niece, Suzie, after graduating with a BA in economics, began work for an investment company in New York. My nephew, Eric, got married in 2018. He and his wife, Jessie, bought a house in Dallas, and Eric is working for the company Jessie's father founded.

Sam and his family moved from Houston to Los Angeles in 1984. Until his retirement in 2017, Sam was a successful auto body shop owner. Janet works for a civil engineering company and is looking forward to retiring in the coming years. Both of their kids live in the Los Angeles area. Len is in the real estate business and recently got engaged. Mila became a registered nurse and is studying to become a nurse practitioner. She is married to Robert and has three wonderful kids—Ariel, Natalia, and Michael.

After trying very hard to adjust to Texas, in 1988 Sophia's parents moved to West Hollywood, where a very large Jewish Russian-speaking population resided. They became very independent and had a pretty happy life there. Sophia's dad passed away in 2003. Sophia's mom is ninety years old and, with help, still resides in her own apartment.

In 1997 Sophia and I decided to make a very bold move of purchasing a house in one of the most prestigious Fort Worth neighborhoods, the gated community around a championship golf course. It proved to be a very good move, and today, we still live there.

I have been involved with different Jewish organizations, serving on the board of directors for most of them.

When in 1996 I discovered that there was an active B'nai B'rith Lodge in Fort Worth, my dad's words about this organization quickly made my decision to join it. I have been serving on the board of directors for the Lodge since joining it and twice was elected as its president.

In addition, I have served as president of the B'nai B'rith apartments, a one hundred plus apartment building for low-income seniors of all religions. I still serve on the board almost fifteen years later. At the peak of the Jewish Russian immigration, between 1990 and 2010, there were over thirty elderly Jewish Russian-speaking seniors living in the apartments.

For me, it was a great satisfaction that I was in a position to help the elderly Russian Jews. Most of them had been through the war with Germany and had faced anti-

Semitism, so making their lives more comfortable meant a lot.

I have also served on the board of the Jewish Federation, and for two years I chaired the Jewish Family Service organization.

In 2012 as recognition of my volunteering, I was named as and presented with the Jewish Person of the Year award. It was a very rewarding moment in my life. It happened during the yearly dinner event, and it was a total surprise. Looking at Sophia, my sister, and more than 160 people attending the dinner made me feel very proud of what we have achieved in America during such a short time. And most importantly, we did it ourselves.

I want to finish my story by saying that almost everything in our lives is possible to achieve and accomplish.

Most likely each person will face tremendous obstacles during their life. They may include personal, social, or other issues we feel are out of our control.

After reading my story, you probably noticed that all of the obstacles I mentioned, we faced and overcame.

It can be very hard and feel impossible to make it through some of them, and some of them can be breezed through.

Regardless of the problems you may face, never say the words "it's too hard, I give up".

Keep in mind that it's not just you who may lose or who may suffer from your giving up.

It always works the same way as a passage from the Talmud teaches us: "Whoever saves a life, it's as if one saves the entire world."

There were many more details and stories in our journey. I feel that the most important message was delivered just through the ones I included.

I hope our kids, should they be interested in continuing this, will take over from here and tell their stories about growing up in a first generation immigrant family.

Sophia, me, Michael

Sophia, Michael, Robby, me
Sophia's Mom, Sophia's Dad

Sam, me
Janet, Sophia

Suzie, Michael, Polina, Eric, Jessie

Michael, Robert
Ariel, Natalia, Mila

1981 - 2000
Mila, Robby, Len - 19 years later

Sophia, Michael, Polina, me

Our family
Max, me, Robby, Natalia, Diane, Sophia, Michael

Made in the USA
San Bernardino, CA
18 June 2019